THIS BOOK BELONGS TO

The Library of

....

Did you like my book? I pondered it severely before releasing this book. Although the response has been overwhelming, it is always pleasing to see, read or hear a new comment. Thank you for reading this and I would love to hear your honest opinion about it. Furthermore, many people are searching for a unique book, and your feedback will help me gather the right books for my reading audience.

Thanks!

Table of Contents

Introduction   24

Chapter 1–Beach Crochet Bags   25

Pattern 01: Cutest Beach Bag   25

Pattern 02: Triple Pattern Beach Bag   27

Chapter 2–Summer Crochet Bags   30

Pattern 03: Sling Pattern for Summer   30

Pattern 04: Flower Crochet Bag   32

Chapter 3–Crochet Clutch Bags   37

Pattern 05: Cash and Card Case   37

Pattern 06: Emerald Clutch   38

Chapter 4–Flowery Crochet Patterns   42

Pattern 07: Flower Crochet Bag   42

Pattern 08: Roses Tote   45

Chapter 5–Crochet Pouch Bags   47

Pattern 09: Pineapple Pouch   47

Pattern 10: Draw String Crochet Bag   50

Conclusion   53

Crochet Book Covers   54

15 Wonderful Crochet Patterns To Cover Your Books   54

Introduction   55

Chapter 1–The Basics   57

Zig Zag Zipper   57

Owl's Eyes Cover   58

Blue And Gold Besties   59

Chapter 2–Cute As a Button   61

Green Striped Goodness   62

Meadow Madness   63

Chapter 3–Just What You Wanted   65

Handy Handle   65

The Lady of Lace   66

Crazy Days   67

Chapter 4–Books and Books 69

Multi-Goodness Goddess 69

Pleased as a Plum 70

Green Machine 71

Chapter 5–The Best of the Rest 73

The Pretty Pastel 73

Rainbow Valley Beauty Book 74

The Scholar Cover 75

Chapter 6–Making It Your Own 77

Conclusion 79

Crochet Mandala: 80

12 Most Gorgeous Patterns With Easy Instructions 80

Introduction 81

Chapter 1–12 Most Gorgeous Patterns With Easy Instructions 82

Pattern 01: Blooming Mandala 82

Pattern 02: Flower Madala 86

Pattern 03: Mandala Beanie 87

Pattern 04: Crochet Doily 91

Pattern 05: Spring Rug 93

Pattern 06: Colorful Mini Mandala 96

Pattern 07: Flower Mandala 97

Pattern 08: Black Mandala 98

Pattern 09: Mandala Blanket 100

Pattern 10: Mandala Pouch 103

Pattern 11: Mandala Bag for Market 106

Pattern 12: Mandala Shoulder Bag 109

Conclusion 111

Crochet Pillow: 112

10 Brilliant Crochet Pillow Cases To Make Your Home Super Cozy 112
Introduction 113
Design no. 1 Checkerboard Pillow crochet Pattern 116
Design no. 2 Circular pillow at top 119
Design no. 3 Second round pillow 121

Design no. 4 Square Yellow Pillow   123

Design no. 5   125

Design no. 6 Diagonal pillow   127

Design no. 7   129

Design no. 8 Simple Round pillow   131

Design no. 9 Ribbon laced crochet cushion   133

Design no. 10   137

Conclusion   139

SUMMARY

The Art and Utility of Everyday Crochet: The Art and Utility of Everyday Crochet is a comprehensive guide that delves into the world of crochet, exploring its artistic aspects as well as its practical applications in everyday life. This book is a must-have for both beginners and experienced crocheters, as it offers a wealth of information, tips, and inspiration.

The author takes the reader on a journey through the history of crochet, tracing its origins and evolution over the years. From its humble beginnings as a craft practiced by women in their homes to its current status as a popular form of self-expression, crochet has come a long way. The book explores the various techniques and stitches used in crochet, providing step-by-step instructions and detailed illustrations to help readers master the art.

But this book goes beyond just teaching the basics of crochet. It delves into the creative possibilities that crochet offers, showcasing the work of talented artists who have pushed the boundaries of the craft. From intricate lacework to bold and colorful designs, the book showcases a wide range of crochet projects that will inspire readers to unleash their creativity.

In addition to its artistic merits, crochet also has numerous practical applications. The book explores how crochet can be used to create a variety of useful items for the home, such as blankets, pillows, and rugs. It also delves into the world of fashion, showcasing how crochet can be used to create stylish garments and accessories. Whether you're looking to spruce up your living space or add a unique touch to your wardrobe, this book provides plenty of ideas and inspiration.

The Art and Utility of Everyday Crochet also addresses the therapeutic benefits of crochet. Many people find the repetitive motions of crochet to be calming and meditative, providing a much-needed escape from the stresses of everyday life. The book explores how crochet can be used as a form of self-care, promoting relaxation and mindfulness.

Overall, The Art and Utility of Everyday Crochet is a comprehensive guide that celebrates the beauty and versatility of crochet. Whether you're a beginner looking to learn the basics or an experienced crocheter seeking new inspiration, this book has something for everyone. With its detailed instructions, stunning illustrations, and insightful commentary, it is sure to become a beloved resource for crochet enthusiasts everywhere.

Navigating Through Patterns, Projects, and Techniques in Crochet: Navigating Through Patterns, Projects, and Techniques in Crochet is a comprehensive guide that aims to provide crocheters of all skill levels with a wealth of knowledge and inspiration. Whether you are a beginner looking to learn the basics or an experienced crocheter seeking new patterns and techniques, this book has something for everyone.

The book begins with an introduction to the art of crochet, covering the history, tools, and materials needed to get started. It then delves into the fundamental stitches and techniques, providing step-by-step instructions and clear illustrations to ensure that even beginners can follow along.

Once the basics are covered, the book progresses to more advanced techniques, such as colorwork, lace, and cables. Each technique is explained in detail, with tips and tricks to help you master them. The book also includes a variety of projects that showcase these techniques, allowing you to practice and apply what you have learned.

One of the highlights of this book is the extensive collection of patterns. From simple scarves and hats to intricate blankets and garments, there is a pattern to suit every taste and skill level. Each pattern is accompanied by detailed instructions, stitch diagrams, and full-color photographs, making it easy to follow along and create beautiful crochet pieces.

In addition to the patterns and techniques, the book also includes helpful tips and advice on choosing yarns, reading patterns, and troubleshooting common issues. There is also a section on finishing techniques, such as blocking and weaving in ends, to ensure that your projects have a polished and professional look.

Whether you are looking to expand your crochet skills, find new project ideas, or simply enjoy the art of crochet, Navigating Through Patterns, Projects, and Techniques in Crochet is a must-have resource. With its comprehensive content, clear instructions, and beautiful designs, this book is sure to become a beloved companion for crocheters everywhere.

What to Expect from This Collection in Crochet: In this collection of crochet patterns, you can expect to find a wide variety of projects that cater to different skill levels and interests. Whether you are a beginner looking to learn new stitches or an experienced crocheter seeking a challenge, there is something for everyone in this collection.

The patterns in this collection are carefully curated to provide a diverse range of projects, including garments, accessories, home decor items, and more. From cozy sweaters and stylish hats to elegant shawls and intricate afghans, you will find patterns that suit your personal style and preferences.

One of the highlights of this collection is the detailed instructions provided for each pattern. Whether you are a visual learner or prefer written instructions, you will find both in this collection. The step-by-step instructions are accompanied by clear and concise diagrams and charts, making it easy for you to follow along and create beautiful crochet pieces.

Additionally, this collection includes tips and tricks to help you improve your crochet skills. From techniques for achieving perfect tension to suggestions for choosing the right yarn and hook size, you will find valuable information that will enhance your crochet journey.

Furthermore, this collection features a variety of yarns and color combinations, allowing you to customize each project to your liking. Whether you prefer vibrant and bold colors or subtle and muted tones, you will find inspiration in this collection to create unique and eye-catching crochet pieces.

Lastly, this collection aims to inspire creativity and encourage crocheters to think outside the box. While the patterns provided are a great starting point, you are encouraged to experiment with different stitches, yarns, and embellishments to make each project your own. The possibilities are endless, and this collection serves as a springboard for your own creative exploration in the world of crochet.

In conclusion, this collection of crochet patterns offers a diverse range of projects, detailed instructions, helpful tips, and endless possibilities for customization. Whether you are a beginner or an experienced crocheter, this collection is sure to provide hours of enjoyment and inspiration as you create beautiful and unique crochet pieces.

Understanding Crochet: Tools, Materials, and Stitches: Understanding Crochet: Tools, Materials, and Stitches is a comprehensive guide that aims to provide readers with a thorough understanding of the art of crochet. Whether you are a beginner looking to learn the basics or an experienced crocheter seeking to expand your skills, this book has something to offer for everyone.

The book starts by introducing the essential tools needed for crochet. From crochet hooks of various sizes to stitch markers and tapestry needles, the author explains the purpose and usage of each tool in detail. This section also covers the different types of yarns available and how to choose the right yarn for your projects. The author provides valuable tips on yarn weight, fiber content, and color selection, ensuring that readers have a solid foundation in selecting the appropriate materials for their crochet endeavors.

Moving on, the book delves into the various stitches used in crochet. Starting with the basic stitches such as chain stitch, single crochet, and double crochet, the author provides step-by-step instructions accompanied by clear illustrations. As the book progresses, more advanced stitches like treble crochet, shell stitch, and popcorn stitch are introduced, allowing readers to gradually build their repertoire of crochet stitches. The author also includes helpful tips and tricks for achieving even tension and consistent stitch size, ensuring that readers can create beautifully finished projects.

In addition to teaching the fundamental stitches, Understanding Crochet: Tools, Materials, and Stitches also explores different crochet techniques. From working in the round to creating intricate lace patterns, the book covers a wide range of techniques that will inspire readers to take their crochet skills to the next level. The author provides detailed explanations and visual aids to guide readers through each technique, making it easy to follow along and master new crochet skills.

To further enhance the learning experience, the book includes a variety of crochet patterns for readers to practice their newfound skills. From simple scarves and hats to more complex blankets and garments, the author offers a diverse selection of patterns suitable for crocheters of all levels. Each pattern is accompanied by clear instructions, stitch diagrams, and full-color photographs, ensuring that readers can successfully complete their projects with confidence.

It is a comprehensive resource that empowers readers to explore their creativity and express themselves through crochet. With its detailed explanations, helpful tips, and inspiring patterns, this book is a must-have for anyone interested in the art of crochet. Whether you are a beginner or an experienced crocheter,

Basic Techniques and Stitches: A Refresher in Crochet:

A Comprehensive Refresher in Crochet

Are you a crochet enthusiast who wants to brush up on your skills and expand your knowledge of basic techniques and stitches? Look no further! In this comprehensive refresher course, we will delve into the world of crochet and explore a wide range of techniques and stitches that will take your crochet projects to the next level.

Crochet is a versatile craft that allows you to create beautiful and intricate designs using just a hook and yarn. Whether you're a beginner looking to learn the basics or an experienced crocheter wanting to refine your skills, this refresher course is designed to cater to all skill levels.

We will start by revisiting the fundamental techniques that form the foundation of crochet. From holding the hook and yarn correctly to creating a slip knot and foundation chain, we will ensure that you have a solid understanding of the basics before moving on to more advanced stitches.

Once we have covered the basics, we will dive into the world of stitches. From the classic single crochet and double crochet to more complex stitches like the treble crochet and shell stitch, you will learn how to create a variety of textures and patterns in your crochet projects. We will explore the different uses and applications of each stitch, allowing you to choose the perfect stitch for your next project.

In addition to learning individual stitches, we will also cover techniques such as increasing and decreasing stitches, working in the round, and joining motifs. These techniques are essential for creating seamless and professional-looking crochet projects, and we will guide you through each step with detailed instructions and helpful tips.

Throughout the course, you will have the opportunity to practice your newly acquired skills through a series of hands-on projects. From simple dishcloths and scarves to more intricate blankets and garments, these projects will allow you to apply the techniques and stitches you have learned in a practical and creative way.

By the end of this refresher course, you will have a solid understanding of basic crochet techniques and stitches, as well as the confidence to tackle more complex projects. Whether you want to create beautiful gifts for your loved ones or start your own crochet business, this course will equip you with the skills and knowledge you need to succeed.

So, grab your hook and yarn, and get ready to embark on a crochet journey like no other. Join us in this comprehensive refresher course and unlock your full crochet potential!

Decoding Crochet Patterns and Symbols: This is a comprehensive guide that aims to demystify the intricate world of crochet patterns and symbols. Whether you are a beginner or an experienced crocheter, this guide will provide you with the necessary knowledge and skills to understand and interpret crochet patterns with ease.

Crochet patterns are essentially a set of instructions that guide you through the process of creating a specific crochet project. However, these patterns can often be overwhelming, especially for beginners, due to the use of various symbols and abbreviations. This guide breaks down these symbols and abbreviations, explaining their meanings and how they are used in crochet patterns.

The guide begins by introducing the basic crochet stitches and techniques, ensuring that even those who are new to crochet can follow along. It then progresses to explain the different types of crochet patterns, such as written patterns, charts, and diagrams. Each type is thoroughly explained, with step-by-step instructions on how to read and understand them.

One of the main focuses of this guide is decoding crochet symbols. Crochet patterns often use symbols to represent different stitches and techniques, which can be confusing for those who are not familiar with them. This guide provides a comprehensive list of commonly used crochet symbols, along with their corresponding stitch or technique. It also includes detailed explanations and illustrations to help you understand how each symbol is used in a pattern.

In addition to decoding symbols, this guide also covers other important aspects of crochet patterns, such as gauge, sizing, and pattern repeats. Understanding these elements is crucial for achieving the desired outcome of your crochet project. The guide provides clear explanations and examples, ensuring that you can confidently apply these concepts to any crochet pattern you encounter.

Furthermore, this guide offers tips and tricks for troubleshooting common issues that may arise while following crochet patterns. It addresses common mistakes, such as miscounting stitches or misinterpreting symbols, and provides solutions to help you overcome these challenges.

Decoding Crochet Patterns and Symbols is not just a reference book, but a comprehensive learning tool that empowers you to confidently tackle any crochet pattern. With its detailed explanations, illustrations, and practical examples, this guide will enhance your crochet skills and enable you to create beautiful and intricate crochet projects. Whether you aspire to crochet intricate lace shawls or cozy blankets, this guide will be your go-to resource for deciphering crochet patterns and symbols.

Choosing the Right Yarn and Colors in Crochet: Choosing the right yarn and colors in crochet is an important aspect of any crochet project. The yarn you choose can greatly impact the final look and feel of your project, while the colors you select can enhance or detract from the overall design. Therefore, it is crucial to carefully consider these factors before starting any crochet project.

When it comes to selecting the right yarn, there are several factors to consider. First and foremost, you need to think about the type of project you are working on. Different projects require different types of yarn, such as cotton for dishcloths or wool for warm winter accessories. It is important to choose a yarn that is suitable for the intended purpose of your project.

Another important factor to consider is the weight or thickness of the yarn. Yarns come in various weights, ranging from super fine to super bulky. The weight of the yarn will determine the size of the stitches and the overall drape of your project. For example, if you are making a delicate lace shawl, you would want to choose a fine weight yarn, whereas if you are making a cozy blanket, a bulky weight yarn would be more appropriate.

Additionally, the fiber content of the yarn is also important to consider. Different fibers have different properties, such as warmth, durability, and softness. Some common yarn fibers include acrylic, cotton, wool, and alpaca. Each fiber has its own unique characteristics, so it is important to choose a fiber that aligns with your project requirements and personal preferences.

In addition to selecting the right yarn, choosing the right colors is equally important in crochet. The colors you choose can greatly impact the overall look and feel of your project. When selecting colors, it is important to consider the intended purpose of your project, as well as your personal style and preferences.

One approach to selecting colors is to consider the color theory. Color theory involves understanding how different colors interact with each other and how they can create different moods or effects. For example, complementary colors (colors that are opposite each other on the color wheel) can create a vibrant and eye-catching effect, while analogous colors (colors that are next to each other on the color wheel) can create a harmonious and soothing effect.

Another approach to selecting colors is to consider the color palette or theme of your project. You can choose a monochromatic color scheme, where you use different shades and tints of the same color, or you can opt for a more vibrant and contrasting color scheme.

Exploring Different Crochet Stitches and Their Textures: When it comes to crochet, there is a wide variety of stitches that can be used to create different textures and patterns in your projects. Whether you are a beginner or an experienced crocheter, exploring different crochet stitches can add depth and interest to your work.

One of the most basic crochet stitches is the single crochet stitch. This stitch creates a dense and sturdy fabric, making it perfect for items like dishcloths or blankets. It is worked by inserting the hook into the stitch, yarn over, and pulling through both loops on the hook. The single crochet stitch can be used on its own or in combination with other stitches to create different patterns.

Another commonly used stitch is the double crochet stitch. This stitch is taller than the single crochet stitch and creates a looser and more open fabric. It is worked by yarn over, inserting the hook into the stitch, yarn over again, and pulling through the first two loops on the hook. The double crochet stitch is great for creating lacy patterns or garments with a more lightweight feel.

If you are looking for a stitch that adds texture to your crochet projects, the popcorn stitch is a great option. This stitch creates small, raised bumps on the fabric, giving it a three-dimensional look. It is worked by making several double crochet stitches in the same stitch or space, then removing the hook from the loop and inserting it into the first double crochet made. The loop is then pulled through all the stitches on the hook, creating a popcorn effect.

For a more intricate and delicate texture, the shell stitch is a popular choice. This stitch is made by working a series of double crochet stitches in the same stitch or space, then skipping a certain number of stitches before repeating the pattern. The result is a scalloped edge or shell-like pattern that adds elegance to any project.

In addition to these stitches, there are countless other crochet stitches that can be explored and combined to create unique textures and patterns. Some examples include the treble crochet stitch, the half double crochet stitch, and the cluster stitch. Each stitch has its own characteristics and can be used to achieve different effects in your crochet work.

Exploring different crochet stitches not only allows you to create visually interesting projects, but it also helps to expand your crochet skills and knowledge. By trying out new stitches and experimenting with different combinations, you can develop your own style and create truly one-of-a-kind pieces.

So, whether you are a beginner looking to learn new stitches or an experienced

Understanding Gauge and Adjusting Patterns in Crochet:

Crocheting is a popular craft that allows individuals to create beautiful and intricate designs using yarn and a crochet hook. However, one of the most important aspects of crocheting is understanding gauge and how to adjust patterns accordingly. Gauge refers to the number of stitches and rows per inch in a crocheted fabric, and it plays a crucial role in ensuring that the finished project turns out the way it is intended.

When starting a crochet project, it is essential to check the gauge specified in the pattern. This is usually indicated by a small swatch of crocheted fabric that is measured to determine the number of stitches and rows per inch. The gauge is typically given in a specific stitch pattern, such as single crochet or double crochet, and using the recommended hook size. By comparing your own gauge to the pattern's gauge, you can determine if your tension and stitch size match the designer's intentions.

If your gauge does not match the pattern's gauge, adjustments will need to be made to ensure that the finished project turns out the correct size. If your gauge is too loose, meaning you have fewer stitches and rows per inch than the pattern calls for, you will need to switch to a smaller hook size to achieve a tighter tension. Conversely, if your gauge is too tight, with more stitches and rows per inch than the pattern specifies, you will need to switch to a larger hook size to create a looser tension.

Adjusting the gauge can be a bit of trial and error, as it may take a few swatches and hook size changes to achieve the desired measurements. It is important to remember that the hook size is not the only factor that affects gauge. The type of yarn used, the individual's tension, and even the time of day can all impact the gauge. Therefore, it is crucial to be patient and willing to experiment until the correct gauge is achieved.

Once the gauge has been adjusted to match the pattern, it is important to continue checking it throughout the project. This is especially true for larger projects, such as blankets or garments, where even a slight variation in gauge can result in a significantly different finished size. By periodically measuring the gauge as you work, you can ensure that your tension remains consistent and that the final product will meet your expectations.

In conclusion, understanding gauge and adjusting patterns in crochet is essential for achieving the desired size and fit of your finished projects.

Introducing More Advanced Stitches and Techniques in Crochet: In this crochet tutorial, we will be delving into the world of more advanced stitches and techniques. If you have mastered the basic stitches like single crochet, double crochet, and half double crochet, then you are ready to take your crochet skills to the next level.

One of the first advanced stitches we will explore is the treble crochet stitch. This stitch is taller than the double crochet and creates a more open and lacy fabric. To work a treble crochet, you will yarn over twice before inserting your hook into the designated stitch. Then, yarn over and pull through two loops on your hook, repeating this step two more times until you have one loop left on your hook. This stitch is great for creating intricate lace patterns or adding height to your projects.

Another advanced stitch we will cover is the popcorn stitch. This stitch creates a raised, textured effect that adds dimension to your crochet work. To make a popcorn stitch, you will work a set number of double crochets into the same stitch, but instead of completing each stitch, you will leave the last loop of each stitch on your hook. Once you have completed the required number of stitches, you will yarn over and pull through all the loops on your hook, securing them together. This stitch is perfect for creating decorative elements or adding visual interest to your projects.

In addition to learning new stitches, we will also explore advanced techniques such as colorwork and shaping. Colorwork involves using multiple colors of yarn to create intricate patterns or designs within your crochet work. This technique can be achieved through techniques like tapestry crochet, where you carry the unused color along the back of your work, or through intarsia crochet, where you work with separate bobbins of yarn for each color. Colorwork adds a beautiful and eye-catching element to your projects.

Shaping is another important technique to master in crochet. It involves increasing or decreasing stitches to create curves, angles, or tailored fits in your projects. Techniques like increasing through adding extra stitches or decreasing through skipping stitches can be used to shape garments, accessories, or amigurumi. Understanding how to shape your crochet work will allow you to create more professional-looking and well-fitting finished pieces.

As you delve into more advanced stitches and techniques in crochet, it is important to remember to practice and be patient with yourself. These skills may take time to master, but with dedication and perseverance, you will be able to create beautiful and intricate crochet projects.

Understanding the Principles of Design in Crochet: Understanding the principles of design in crochet is essential for creating beautiful and visually appealing projects. Whether you are a beginner or an experienced crocheter, having a solid understanding of these principles will help you make informed decisions about color, texture, shape, and overall composition.

One of the key principles of design in crochet is color theory. Understanding how colors interact with each other can greatly enhance the visual impact of your crochet projects. You can create different moods and effects by using complementary colors (colors that are opposite each other on the color wheel) or analogous colors (colors that are next to each other on the color wheel). Additionally, understanding the concept of value (the lightness or darkness of a color) and saturation (the intensity or purity of a color) can help you create depth and dimension in your crochet work.

Texture is another important aspect of design in crochet. By using different stitches and techniques, you can create a variety of textures in your projects. For example, using a combination of single crochet and double crochet stitches can create a bumpy or raised texture, while using a combination of puff stitches and picot stitches can create a more lacy and delicate texture. Understanding how to manipulate stitches and combine different textures can add interest and visual appeal to your crochet projects.

Shape and form are also fundamental principles of design in crochet. By varying the size and shape of your stitches, you can create different shapes and forms in your projects. For example, using increases and decreases can create curves and angles, while using different stitch patterns can create geometric shapes. Understanding how to manipulate stitches and create different shapes can help you achieve the desired look and structure in your crochet projects.

Lastly, the overall composition of your crochet project is crucial in design. Composition refers to how the elements of your project are arranged and organized. Consideration should be given to the placement of colors, textures, and shapes to create a balanced and visually pleasing composition. This can be achieved through careful planning and experimentation, as well as considering the intended purpose and function of the project.

In conclusion, understanding the principles of design in crochet is essential for creating visually appealing and well-executed projects. By considering color theory, texture, shape, and overall composition, you can elevate your crochet work to a new level. Whether you are creating a simple scarf or a complex garment, applying these principles will help you achieve the desired aesthetic and make your crochet projects truly stand out.

Translating Ideas into Stitches and Rows in Crochet: Crochet, a popular craft that involves creating fabric by interlocking loops of yarn with a hooked needle, offers endless possibilities for translating ideas into stitches and rows. Whether you're a beginner or an experienced crocheter, the process of transforming your creative ideas into tangible crochet projects can be both exciting and rewarding.

To begin, it's important to have a clear vision of what you want to create. This could be anything from a cozy blanket to a stylish sweater, a cute amigurumi toy, or even a decorative item for your home. Once you have a specific idea in mind, you can start breaking it down into smaller components and determining the stitches and techniques that will bring your vision to life.

One of the first steps in translating your idea into stitches is choosing the right yarn. Yarn comes in various weights, textures, and colors, each offering a unique look and feel to your finished project. Consider the desired drape, warmth, and texture of your item when selecting the yarn. For example, a soft and bulky yarn would be perfect for a cozy winter scarf, while a lightweight and breathable yarn would be more suitable for a summer top.

Next, you'll need to select the appropriate crochet hook size. The size of your hook will determine the size and tension of your stitches. A larger hook will create looser and more open stitches, while a smaller hook will result in tighter and denser stitches. It's important to match the hook size to the recommended gauge provided in your pattern or to the desired outcome of your project.

Once you have your yarn and hook ready, it's time to start crocheting. Depending on your idea, you may need to learn or brush up on specific crochet stitches and techniques. Basic stitches like single crochet, double crochet, and treble crochet are the building blocks of most crochet projects. However, there are countless other stitches and techniques that can add texture, color, and complexity to your work.

As you begin stitching, it's helpful to have a pattern or a rough sketch of your project to guide you. Patterns provide step-by-step instructions, stitch counts, and diagrams to ensure accuracy and consistency in your work. If you're feeling more adventurous, you can also experiment with creating your own patterns or modifying existing ones to suit your vision.

Throughout the process, it's important to stay patient and practice. Crocheting requires precision and attention to detail, but with time and practice, you'll become more comfortable and confident in your

Testing and Adjusting Your Own Patterns in Crochet: Testing and adjusting your own patterns in crochet is an essential skill for any crocheter who wants to create unique and well-fitting designs. Whether you're designing a garment, an accessory, or even a home decor item, being able to test and adjust your patterns will ensure that your finished project turns out just the way you envisioned it.

The first step in testing your crochet pattern is to make a sample swatch. This swatch should be worked in the same stitch pattern and with the same yarn and hook size that you plan to use for your project. By making a swatch, you can get a sense of how the stitch pattern looks and feels, as well as how it drapes and stretches. This will help you determine if any adjustments need to be made to the stitch count or hook size.

Once you have your swatch, it's time to start testing your pattern. Follow the instructions exactly as written, making note of any issues or inconsistencies that you come across. Pay attention to things like stitch count, stitch placement, and any special instructions or techniques. If you find that the stitch count is off or that the pattern doesn't seem to be working up correctly, it may be necessary to make adjustments.

When making adjustments to your pattern, it's important to keep track of what changes you're making and why. This will help you remember what adjustments you've already tried and will make it easier to troubleshoot any issues that arise. Some common adjustments you may need to make include adding or subtracting stitches, changing the stitch pattern, or adjusting the size or shape of the project.

After making your adjustments, it's time to test the pattern again. Work through the revised instructions, paying close attention to how the changes you made affect the overall design. If you're happy with the results, you can move on to making your project. However, if you're still not satisfied, don't be afraid to make further adjustments and test the pattern again. It may take several rounds of testing and adjusting before you achieve the desired outcome.

In addition to testing and adjusting your own patterns, it's also helpful to have others test your patterns as well. This can provide valuable feedback and help identify any issues or areas for improvement that you may have missed. Consider joining a crochet group or online community where you can share your patterns and ask for feedback. You can also consider hiring a professional pattern tester who can provide detailed feedback and suggestions for improvement.

Introduction

Each successful project will help you to increase your self-esteem and self-expression. With constant practice, you will be able to build new crocheting skills. This new skill will help you to deal with the fear of unemployment because you can earn money by selling crocheted projects. Several studies show that crafting can postpone or reduce dementia. Dementia is related to memory loss with age.

This book has 10 interesting crochet bag patterns for you to try.

Chapter 1 – Beach Crochet Bags

If you want beautiful beach crochet bags, there are two patterns for you. These are extremely easy and beautiful:

Pattern 01: Cutest Beach Bag

- **Crochet Hook:** 5mm or H/8
- **Weight of Yarn:** (5) Chunky/Bulky (12 to 15 stitches for four inches)
- Red Ribbon: 4 to 5 skeins (7/8" width)
- Safety pin or stitch marker
- Red thread and needle

Pattern:

Start with base

Chain 36.

Row 1 to 13: Single crochet into every of the 36 chain, chain 1, and flip.

Row 14: Single crochet in the subsequent 35 single crochet, 3 single crochet in the subsequent single crochet at the closing of the row (i.e. 36 single crochet stitch) (this will be the first corner, single crochet in the stitches to make the width of your bag (about 12 single crochet), 3 in the previous stitch that makes up the width (2nd corner) and you are on the opposite side of the length of foundation where you have chained 36. Single crochet in every of the subsequent 35 stitch, 3 single crochet in the subsequent single crochet at the closing of the row (i.e. 36 chain stitch) (This will again make the 3rd corner), single crochet in the stitches to make width of bag (about 12 single crochet), 3 in the preceding stitch for width and slip stitch to seam the beginning row.

Get Ready to Construct Body of Bag:

Row 15: Chain 1, single crochet in the Back Loop only in every single crochet in the round. Slip stitch to seam round.

Row 16: Chain 1, single crochet in both loops in every single crochet in the round. Slip stitch to seam round.

Row 17,21,25,29,33,37: Chain 3 (counts 1 double crochet), double crochet in both loops in every single crochet in the round. Slip stitch to seam round.

Row 18,22,26,30,34,38: Chain 1, single crochet in both loops in every double crochet in the round. Slip stitch to seam round.

Row 19,23,27,31,35: Chain 4 (consider as 1 double crochet and chain 1), skip single crochet, *double crochet in the subsequent single crochet, chain 1, skip the subsequent single crochet, ** replicate * to ** 54 x, slip stitch to seam round.

Row 20,24,28,32,36: chain 1, single crochet in every space in the round. Slip stitch to seam round.

Design Shoulder Straps:

Put the bag flat and measure 5" on your right & left closing of this bag and mark with one stitch marker or use a safety pin. You can replicate this on the other side of the bag. The 5" marker is the center of every strap. There will be 4 stitch markers (2 on every side of your bag) Crochet the straps with the help of given pattern:

*Row 1: Slip stitch into the single crochet that 2.5" from the closing of the bag and the stitch marker. Chain 1, single crochet in the subsequent 7 single crochet. (you will need stitch marker to do this).

Row 2: 1 chain, single crochet in the subsequent 3 single crochet, chain 1, skip subsequent single crochet, single crochet in the subsequent 3 single crochet.

The pattern for (Odd numbered) Rows: Single crochet in the subsequent single crochet.

The pattern for (Even number) Rows: Chain, single crochet in the subsequent 3 single crochet, chain 1, skip subsequent single crochet, single crochet in the subsequent 3 single crochet.

You have to replicate both odd and even rows until you get total 77 rows. Single crochet the strap to 2nd closing of your bag on the similar side of the bag. Make sure to keep the middle strap to its place with another stitch marker. Take off your stitch marker to complete your work. ** Replicate from * to ** for the second side of this bag.

Adding the Ribbon Embellishment

You will create gaps in the body for 19, 23, 27, 31 and 35. You will add ribbons in this gap.

Step 1: Safety pin your ribbon to its place where you started to create tension. You need to weave horizontally from outside to inside in the gaps. If the ribbon fills gap on 1 row, you can move ribbon without cutting. There is no need to cut because cutting can mess up everything and you will have to stitch it later. Fill al gaps in the body of the bag and if your run out of your skein, close with a safety pin to close one skein and start a new skein of your ribbon.

Step 2: Once you are satisfied with placement, cut off the leftover ribbon and secure hand stitch at all closings.

Step 3: Use a needle to hand-stitch and thread ribbon to the inner side of your bag. There is no need to stitch the long ribbons outside the bags. Embellishment of ribbon for the straps is made in a similar way. You can buy an extra skein of ribbon for both straps and sew ribbons inside of straps at the closing point.

Pattern 02: Triple Pattern Beach Bag

MATERIALS:

- Color A: 3 skeins
- Colors B: 2 skeins

- Color C: 2 skeins
- Color D: 2 skeins
- Size J crochet hook

First Pattern: With Color D, chain 96. Seam with a slip stitch into the ring, careful not to twist chain.

Row 1: Chain 1, work 1 single crochet in same st as seam, * chain 1, skip 1 chain, 1 single crochet in subsequent chain, replicate from * around, chain 1, skip the last chain, drop D; with A, slip stitch to top of first single crochet, chain 1: 48 mesh.

Row 2: With A, work 1 single crochet in the seam, *chain 1, 1 single crochet in subsequent space, replicate from * around, end chain 1; with color D, slip stitch to first single crochet, chain 1.

Row 3: With color D, replicate Row 2.

Replicate Rows 2 and 3 until there are 5 rows of A. Increasing 1 pattern in every 6th pattern, work 1 more row of D, seam and tie up: 56 patterns.

2ND Pattern: Row 1: With loop of B on hook, work 1 single crochet in first st, * 4-double crochet shell in subsequent space, skip subsequent chain-1 space, 1 single crochet in subsequent space, skip subsequent space, replicate from * around, end last 4-double crochet shell in last space, drop B; with C, seam with slip stitch to first single crochet: 14 shells.

Row 2: Chain 3 for first double crochet, work 1 double crochet in the same place as seam, * 1 single crochet in space between 2nd and 3rd double crochet of subsequent shell, 4 double crochet in subsequent single crochet, replicate from * around, end 1 single crochet in middle of the last shell, 2 double crochet in the same place as first 2 double crochet, drop color C; with B, seam.

Row 3: 1 single crochet in the seam, 1 shell in every single crochet and 1 single crochet in the middle of every shell, drop B; with A, seam to first single crochet.

Rows 4 through 7: Continue in shell pattern, working 1 row every of A, B, C and B, seam. Tie up all colors.

3RD PATTERN: Row 1: On the wrong side of one loop of A on hook, work * 2 single crochet in single crochet, 1 single crochet in every of 4 double crochet, replicate from * around, drop A, with C, seam with slip stitch to first single crochet, chain 3, turn: 84 stitches.

Row 2: 2 double crochet in the base of chain-3. * skip 2, work 3 double crochet in subsequent st, replicate from * around, drop C, with A, seam with slip stitch to top of chain-3, turn. 28 shells.

Row 3: * Chain 2, 1 single crochet in the middle of the subsequent shell, replicate from * around, drop A, with C - chain 3, turn.

Rows 4, 5, 6 and 7: Replicate Rows 2 and 3. Tie up C.

Row 8: With A, * work 1 single crochet in subsequent single crochet, 2 single crochet in space, replicate from * around, drop A, with B, slip stitch to first single crochet, chain 2, turn.

4TH Pattern: Row 1: With chain 2 as first half-double-crochet, work 1 more half-double-crochet at the base of chain-2 for the first group, * 2 half-double-crochet in subsequent st, skip 1 st, replicate from * around; 42 half-double-crochet groups; with A, seam, chain 2, turn.

Row 2: With chain-2 as first half-double-crochet work 1 more half-double-crochet in first space for the first group, 2 half-double-crochet in space between every 2-half-double-crochet groups, end 2 half-double-crochet in space before turning-chain, tie up.

Row 3: Seam B in space after 12th group, chain 2, turn, 1 half-double-crochet in same space, 2 half-double-crochet in every of 19 spaces, change to A, chain 2, turn.

Row 4: 2 half-double-crochet in subsequent space and in every space, end 2 half-double-crochet in last space, 1 half-double-crochet in turning chain; change to B, chain 2, turn.

Row 5: 2 half-double-crochet in space between first and 2nd groups, 2 half-double-crochet in every space, end 1 half-double-crochet in turning chain, change to A, chain 2, turn.

Alternating 1 row every of A and B, replicate Row 5 until 4 groups rem.

Subsequent row works two groups, one group in turning chain, chain two, turn.

Still alternating colors, work in the three groups for 9", tie up. With a loop of B on the hook, skip 3 groups on last long row, work two half-double-crochet in subsequent space and work another side the same.

Finishing: Sew ends of handle tog. Seam edges of foundation chain. With C, work 1 row of single crochet around the opening and handle then with D, work 1 row of slip stitches through back loops only. If desired, you can line with felt.

Chapter 2 – Summer Crochet Bags

There are some beautiful summer crochet bags that are easy to crochet with the help of given pattern:

Pattern 03: Sling Pattern for Summer

- Worsted Yarn: 1 ball or more
- Crochet Hook: Size H
- Fabric for Cotton Lining: 1 yd
- Matching thread and needle

Notes:

Chain 3 at the finishing of every row will be counted as the first double crochet of the subsequent row.

Pattern:

Chain 4; join with a slip stitch to form a ring.

Row 1: Chain 3 to count as the first double crochet, work 7 more double crochet in the ring; chain 3, flip. (8 double crochet)

Row 2: Double crochet in the first double crochet, 2 double crochet in every remaining double crochet across; chain 3, flip. (16 double crochet)

Row 3: Replicate row 2. (32 double crochet)

Row 4: Double crochet in the first double crochet and in every double crochet across, 2 double crochet in the top of the flipping chain; chain 3, flip. (34 double crochet) (Increase at every finishing off the row.)

Row 5: Replicate row 4. (36 double crochet)

Row 6: Replicate row 2. (72 double crochet)

Row 7: Replicate row 4. (74 double crochet)

Row 8: Replicate row 4. (76 double crochet)

Row 9: Replicate row 4. (78 double crochet)

Row 10: Replicate row 4. (80 double crochet)

Row 11: Double crochet in the first double crochet (double crochet in the subsequent double crochet, 2 double crochet in the subsequent double crochet) across, double crochet in the flipping chain; chain 3, flip. (120 double crochet)

Row 12: Replicate row 4. (122 double crochet)

Row 13: Replicate row 4. (124 double crochet)

Row 14: Replicate row 4. (126 double crochet)

Row 15: Replicate row 4. (128 double crochet)

Row 16: Replicate row 4. (130 double crochet) Tie up. Weave in all ends.

Handle

Chain 220; being careful not to twist chain, join with a slip stitch to the first chain.

Round 1: Chain 3 to count as the first double crochet, double crochet in every chain around; join with a slip stitch to the top of the beginning chain 3. (220 double crochet)

Round 2: Replicate round 1.

Note: You will need additional yarn if you want to make 5 rows.

Rounds 3 to 5: Replicate round 1.

Assembly

Iron every crocheted part to block. If you want to line your bag, you can lay the crocheted parts of the fabric to trace the pattern of crocheted parts. Make sure to add seam allowance and cut along with traced line. Sew this lining to fit in the bag and flip its inside out. Slip stitch row 16 of one crocheted piece pieces to 130 stitches of row 5 of a handle, then carry on working slip stitch's in the leftover 90 handle stitches; seam with a slip stitch to the initial slip stitch; Tie up. Slip stitch row 16 of the other bag piece to 130 stitches of all free loops of the base chain of this handle, carry on working a slip stitch in the left over 90 handle stitches; seam with a slip stitch to the initial slip stitch; Tie up. Weave its ends.

Insert lining into your bag and whip stitch to the handle and opening of the bag. You can sew inside of the bag, after the initial ring.

Pattern 04: Flower Crochet Bag

- Crochet Hook: 5 mm or H/8
- Weight of Yarn: (4) Aran, Worsted Weight/ Medium Weight (16 to 20 stitches to four inches)

MATERIALS

- Main color (MC): 4 balls
- Color A: 2 balls
- Color B: 2 balls
- Color C: 2 balls
- Color D: 2 balls

Measurements:

Almost 18½" or 47 cm wide X 12½" or 32 cm high.

GAUGE: 14 single crochet and almost 16 rows = 4 inches or 10 cm

Directions:

Motif

With color 1, chain 2.

1st round: 6 single crochet in 2nd chain from hook. Now join with

slip stitch to initial single crochet.

2nd round: Chain 3 (counts as double crochet). 2 double crochet in same space

as last slip stitch. 3 double crochet in every single crochet around. Now join with

slip stitch to top of chain 3. 18 double crochet. Tie up.

Flower: Initial Petal: 1st row: Now join color 2 with slip stitch to front loop only of any double crochet. *Chain 3 (counts as double crochet). 1 double crochet in same space as last slip stitch. 1 double crochet in front loop only of subsequent double crochet. 2 double crochet in front loop only of subsequent double crochet. 5 double crochet for the petal. Flip.

2nd row: Chain 3 (counts as double crochet). 1 double crochet in every double crochet of petal. Flip.

3rd row: Chain 3 (counts as double crochet). (Yarn over hook and draw up a loop in subsequent st. Yarn over hook and draw through 2 loops on hook) 3 times. Yarn over hook and draw through all loops on hook – double crochet3tog made. 1 double crochet in last double crochet. Tie up leaving a long end. *

Second Petal: **Join color 2 again with slip stitch to front loop of subsequent unworked single crochet of 2nd round. Replicate from * to * once. **

Third to Sixth Petals: Replicate from ** to ** 4 times more. 6 petals.

3rd round: Now join color 3 with slip stitch to remaining back loop of any double crochet of 2nd round. Chain 3. 1 double crochet in same space. 2 double crochet in every remaining back loop around. Now join with slip stitch to top of chain 3. 36 double crochet.

4th round: Chain 3. 1 double crochet in same space as last slip stitch. *1 double crochet in subsequent double crochet. 2 double crochet in subsequent double crochet. Replicate from * to last 5 double crochet. 2 double crochet in every of subsequent 4 double crochet. 1 double crochet in last double crochet. Now join with slip stitch to top of chain 3. 56 double crochet.

5th round: Chain 1. 1 single crochet in same space as last slip stitch. 1 single crochet in every of subsequent 4 double crochet. *1 half-double crochet in every of subsequent 2 double crochet. 1 double crochet in every of subsequent 2 double crochet. 5 treble in subsequent double crochet for a corner. 1 double crochet in every of subsequent 2 double crochet. 1 half-double crochet in every of subsequent 2 double crochet. ** 1 single crochet in every of subsequent 5 double crochet. Replicate from * twice more, then from * to ** once.

Now join with slip stitch to initial single crochet.

6th round: Chain 1. 1 single crochet in every stitch around, working 3 single crochet in corners. Now join with slip stitch to initial single crochet. Tie up.

Using yarn ends from every petal, sew around outer edges of petals.

Motif I (make 2)

Using Main Color for color 1, and A for color two and C for 3rd color.

Motif II (make 2)

Use D for 1st color, C for 2nd color and B for 3rd color.

Motif III (make 2)

Use A for 1st color, D for 2nd color and Main Color for 3rd color.

Motif IV (make 2)

Use C for color 1, D for 2nd color and Main Color for 3rd color.

Motif V (make 2)

Use B for color 1, Main Color for 2nd color and A for 3rd color.

Motif VI (make 2)

Use Main Color for color 1, B for 2nd color and C for 3rd color.

Stitch Motifs together as shown in the image for back and front.

Side and Bottom Section

Note: While changing color, make sure to work to previous 2 loops on crochet hook of the last stitch, then pull new color via remaining two loops and continue.

With Main Color, chain 11.

1st row: (Right Side). 1 double crochet in 4th chain from hook (counts as 2 double crochet). 1 double crochet in every chain across. 9 stitches. Now join A. Flip.

2nd row: With A, chain 1. 1 single crochet in every double crochet across. Now join MAIN COLOR. Flip.

3rd row: With MAIN COLOR, chain 3 (consider as double crochet). 1 double crochet in every single crochet across. Now join A. Flip.

4th row: As 2nd row. Now join B. Flip.

5th row: With B, as 3rd row. Now join C. Flip.

6th row: With C, as 2nd row. Now join B. Flip.

7th row: Similar to 5th row.

8th row: With C, as 2nd row. Now join A. Flip.

9th row: With A, as 3rd row. Now join MAIN COLOR. Flip.

10th row: With MAIN COLOR, as 2nd row. Now join A. Flip.

11th row: With A, as 3rd row. Now join Main Color. Flip.

12th row: With MAIN COLOR, as 2nd row. Now join C. Flip.

13th row: With C, as 3rd row. Now join B. Flip.

14th row: With B, as 2nd row. Now join C. Flip.

15th row: With C, as 3rd row. Now join B. Flip.

16th row: With B, as 2nd row. Now join MAIN COLOR. Flip.

17th row: With MAIN COLOR, as 3rd row. Now join A. Flip.

Replicate 2nd to 17th rows until work from beg measures length to fit down one side of Back or Front, across the bottom, then up remaining side. Tie up.

Pin one Side and base Section to the Front and the Back along three sides.

Edging: 1st round: Now join MAIN COLOR with slip stitch in top left corner of Front or Back of Bag. Chain 1. 3 single crochet in same space as slip stitch. Work single crochet equally around, working three single crochet in corners and through both widths where Front and Side sections meet. Now join with slip stitch to initial single crochet.

2nd round: Chain 1. You will work from left side to right, instead of right side to left, as usual, work one reverse single crochet in every single crochet around. Now join with slip stitch to initial single crochet. Tie up.

Replicate border to design back.

Handles (you will make 2)

Start with MAIN COLOR, chain 50.

1st row: (Right Side). 1 double crochet in 4th chain from hook (consider as 2 double crochet). 1 double crochet in every chain across. 48 stitches. Flip.

2nd and 3rd rows: Chain 3 (consider as double crochet). 1 double crochet in every double crochet across. Flip.

Fold Handle in half lengthwise and work 1 row of single crochet through 3rd row and remaining loops of foundation chain. Tie up.

Sew handles as you can see in the picture.

Chapter 3 – Crochet Clutch Bags

There are some stylish clutch bags made of crochet and you can have them in your collection. Try these pattern:

Pattern 05: Cash and Card Case

Crochet Hook: 4mm or G/6 hook
Weight of Yarn: Aran and Worsted/Medium Weight Yarn (4) (16 to 20 stitches to four inches)
Matching Thread
Large Eye Needle

Gauge: 8 single crochet = 2", 7 single crochet = 2"
Chain 15. Read note 1.

ROUND 1: Make 2 single crochet in 2nd chain from hook, single crochet in every chain (12) to last chain, you need to work over the yarn tail for rest of this round, three single crochet in the last chain, work in opposite side of starting chain and single crochet in every of 13 chain stitches; [30 single crochet]

ROUND 2: Slip stitch in BACK loop of first single crochet of round 1 (counts as first single crochet), single crochet in BACK loop of every single crochet around. [30 single crochet] There is no need to join rounds. Read second note.

ROUNDS 3 to 8: Single crochet in BACK loop of subsequent single crochet and in BACK loop of every single crochet around. [30 single crochet]

ROUND 9: Single crochet in BACK loop of subsequent single crochet and in BACK loop of every single crochet around to the last 2 stitches before the side edge fold. Slip stitch in last 2 single crochet ending at the fold. Chain 1, flip.

Now work back and forth in rows.

Row 1: Single crochet in 2 slip stitches, single crochet in 12 single crochet. Chain 1, flip. (14 single crochet)

Row 2: Single crochet in 14 single crochet. (14 single crochet)

Tie up.

Replicate for the second pocket. But do not fasten off after row 2.

Row 3: Keep pockets together with the small side of your pockets on the inner side. Chain 1, single crochet through both pocket upper edges crossways.

Notes!

If you are using multicolor yarn, you will need chain 17 and work almost 10 rows before starting flap. Some multicolor yarns can be thinner than the single color. You need to work 2 rows over 16 stitches.

It looks easy to work the inside case out while working in back loop, flipping the right side out for almost 9 rounds.

Pattern 06: Emerald Clutch

Crochet Hook: 4mm or G/6

Weight of Yarn: Aran and Worsted/Medium Weight (16 to 20 stitches to four inches)

Yarn: Two Skeins in any color almost 75 yards or 50g

Size of Finished Product (when the bag is closed):

Width: 10 inches or 25cm

Height: 5 inches or 14 cm

Buttons: 2

Fabric: Silk Fabric or cotton fabric almost 20 inches. You should select thin fabric; otherwise, the clutch becomes bulky.

Pattern:

Foundation   Chain (ch) 49

Row 1   Ch 1, 1 sc in last ch of the foundation row. Replicate 8 times: [Skip 2, 5 dc in ch st, skip 2, 1 sc in ch st]. Flip.

Row 2   Ch 5, 1 sc in the third dc of the 5 dc cluster in the previous row, ch 2, 1 dc in previous row's sc. Replicate 7 times: [Ch 2, 1 sc in the third dc of the 5 dc cluster in the previous row, ch 2, 1 dc in previous row's sc.] Flip

Row 3   Ch 1, 1 sc in last row's dc. Replicate 8 times: [Skip 2, 5 dc in sc, skip 2, 1 sc into last row's dc st]. Flip

Replicate row 2 & 3 until it measures 30 cm or 12 inches. You will end with one row 2.

Last Row: You can make eyelets to close this clutch.

Ch 1, 1 sc in last row's dc. Skip 2, 5 dc in last row's sc st, skip 2, 1 sc in last row's dc st. Skip 2, 2 dc in last row's sc st, ch 5, 3 dc in same sc st, skip 2, 1 sc in last row's dc st. Replicate 4 times: [Skip 2, 5 dc in previous row's sc st , skip 2, 1 sc in previous row's dc st.] Then you crochet the second eyelet: Skip 2, 3 dc in sc st, ch 5, 2 dc in same sc st, skip 2, 1 sc in last row's dc st. Skip 2, 5 dc in last row's sc st , skip 2, 1 sc in last row's dc st.

Finally, you will cut yarn and weave all ends. See the image:

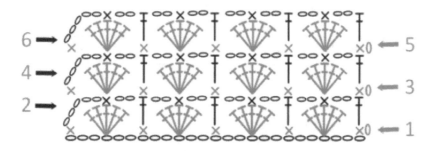

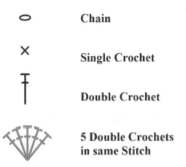

o	Chain
×	Single Crochet
⊤	Double Crochet
	5 Double Crochets in same Stitch

Finished Product:

Sew Button on Fabric:

Sew on the top side of fabric and see the images:

Lining:

Attach fabric of lining like this and then stitch it from inside.

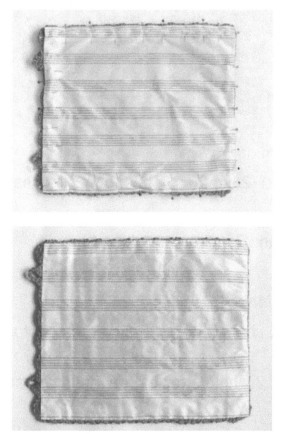

Chapter 4 – Flowery Crochet Patterns

There are a few patterns that are designed with beautiful flowers. You should try these patterns:

Pattern 07: Flower Crochet Bag

Crochet Hook: 3.75 mm or F/5

Weight of Yarn: Fine (2) (23 to 26 stitches to four inches)

1 package yarn

Gauge: 7 inches wide and 7 inches tall without handle

Directions:

Single Layer Flower: (Make 5)

Round 1: With Color A, chain 2. Work 6 single crochet in 2nd chain from hook. Now join. (6 stitches)

Round 2: chain 1. Work 2 single crochet in every stitch around. Now join. Tie up. (12 stitches)

Round 3: Now join Color B. *Chain 3. Work 3 treble or triple crochet in subsequent stitch. Chain 3, slip stitch in subsequent stitch*. Replicate (*) around, for a total of 6 petals. Now join. Tie up.

Round 4: Now join Color C in the top of 1st treble or triple crochet stitch. Chain 1. Single crochet in similar stitch. Single crochet in every of the subsequent 2 treble or triple crochet stitches. Chain 1. *Treble or triple crochet in subsequent slip stitch, between petals. Chain 1. Single crochet in every of the subsequent 3 treble or triple crochet stitches. Chain 1*. Replicate (*) around. Now join.

Round 5: chain 1. Half-double-crochet in similar stitch as Now joining. Half-double-crochet in every of the subsequent 2 single crochet stitches. *Half-double-crochet in chain 1 space. Work {half-double-crochet, chain 2, half-double-crochet} all in subsequent treble or triple crochet stitch. Half-double-crochet in subsequent chain 1 space. Half-double-crochet in every of the subsequent 3 single crochet stitches*. Replicate (*) around, working 1 half-double-crochet in last chain 1 space. Now join. Tie up. Weave in all ends.

Double Layer Flower: (Make 2)

Round 1: With Color A, chain 2. Work 6 single crochet in 2nd chain from hook. Now join. (6 stitches)

Round 2: chain 1. Work 2 single crochet in every stitch around. Now join. Tie up. (12 stitches)

Round 3: Now join Color B. Working in FLO for this round, *Chain 2. Work 2 double crochet in subsequent stitch. Chain 2, slip stitch in subsequent stitch*. Replicate (*) around, for a total of 6 petals. Now join. Slip stitch into an unused back loop of the 1st stitch.

Round 4: Now work in BLO of the similar round~ *Chain 3. Work 3 treble or triple crochet in subsequent stitch. Chain 3, slip stitch in subsequent stitch*. Replicate (*) around, for a total of 6 petals. Now join. Tie up.

Round 5: Now join Color C in the top of 1st treble or triple crochet stitch, of back petals. This entire round is worked in the back petals only, leaving the front petals free. Chain 1. Single crochet in similar stitch. Single crochet in every of the subsequent 2 treble or triple crochet stitches. Chain 1. *Treble or triple crochet in subsequent slip stitch, between petals. Chain 1. Single crochet in every of the subsequent 3 treble or triple crochet stitches. Chain 1*. Replicate (*) around. Now join.

Round 6: chain 1. Half-double-crochet in similar stitch as Now joining. Half-double-crochet in every of the subsequent 2 single crochet stitches. *Half-double-crochet in chain 1 space. Work {half-double-crochet, chain 2, half-double-crochet} all in subsequent treble or triple crochet stitch. Half-double-crochet in subsequent chain 1 space. Half-double-crochet in every of the subsequent 3 single crochet stitches*. Replicate (*) around, working 1 half-double-crochet in last chain 1 space. Now join. Tie up. Weave in all ends.

Handle:

Chain 51. Slip stitch in 2nd chain from hook, and every remaining chain. Tie up, leaving a long tail for sewing.

Now join a contrasting color to either end, and slip stitch in every stitch across. Tie up, leaving a long tail for sewing. (You should have one long tail at every end)

You have to set your motifs as given in the pattern and sew them.

Assembly:

After creating all motifs, you can set them as shown in the picture and stitch them by putting one motif at one time and keep right sides together. You can use any method to stitch. For model, you can slip stitch via BLO for every motif to join them. Put one double layer of motifs in the middle and stitch one single layer motif on each side. One side of motif should touch another motif.

Fold every side half motif, and stitch together.

After stitching front pieces, you can put a second dual layer of motif and stitch right sides to each other. Fold solo motifs in the half to meet the dual layer motif and deal with one at one time and stitch all sides together.

Once it is done, you can weave all ends and flip the side of the bag. Stitch handle by sewing its one end in the chain 2 space at the top part of every side. Weave all ends and the bag is done.

Pattern 08: Roses Tote

Crochet Hook: 4 mm or G/6

Weight of Yarn: Chunky or Super Bulky (6) (4 to 11 stitches for four inches)

MATERIALS:

Premier Yarns

- A: (1 skein)
- B: (1 skein)
- C: (1 skein)
- Thread
- Sewing Needle
- Sixty wooden beads (1 cm)
- Woven tote handles (24 inches wide x 16 inches high)

GAUGE:

8 chains = 4 inches

BAG

Rose (you will make 20 with each color yarn A and B, & C)

Open your yarn and work down to the middle of yarn, insert hook through the center almost 1 1/2" from its end and there will be 1 loop on hook. * insert crochet hook once again through middle of yarn 1" apart (there will be 2 loops on crochet hook), pull 2nd loop on crochet hook through 1st loop on hook – 1 chain form; replicate from * 7 times again. Cut your yarn 1½" from the last chain form, pull a final bit of yarn through the last stitch.

Finishing

* Attach your thread to tie-up end of "A" Rose. Use fingers, coil every Rose into one Rose shape, and pulling out the yarn as you try to make a complete flower. Nail down the middle of the Rose with the help of small stitches and use sewing needle as well as a thread for this purpose. Sew one bead to the middle of each Rose. Sew the "A" Rose to its place on the base of one side of woven tote with numerous stitches. Replicate from * for every Rose, change colors. You have to adjust 12 roses in one row and there are five rows on 24" by 16" tote.

After sewing all roses to your Tote, open sides of all roses with our fingers and fill out their empty spaces one by one. You need needle and thread to manage the edges of roses.

Chapter 5 – Crochet Pouch Bags

You can crochet some pretty pouch bags and there are a few patterns for your assistance:

Pattern 09: Pineapple Pouch

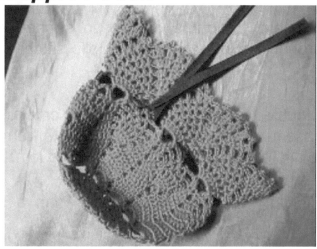

- **Weight of Yarn:** Lace (33 to 40 stitches to four inches) (0)
- **Crochet Thread:** 8 Size Yarn
- **Hook:** Crochet hook of steel 2.20mm or 3 size hook
- **Lace ribbon:** 18 inches long to tie
- **Circumference:** 2 ¾ inches and Height: 3 ¾ inches

Directions:

Special Stitches Instructions:

2dc-bobble: Yo (yarn over), insert crochet hook in stitch and pull yarn thread from side to side, yo and draw through two loops on crochet hook, Yo, put in in similar stitch and pull this thread through, yarn over and draw through two loops on hook, yarn over and draw through all three loops on crochet hook.)

dc2tog: Yarn over, put in crochet hook in stitch and draw thread through, yarn over and pull through two loops on hook, Yarn over, insert in subsequent stitch and drag thread through, yarn over and draw through two loops on crochet hook, yarn over and draw through all three loops on crochet hook.)

Directions:

Use cotton thread of size 8

chain 3 (consider as 1 double crochet).

Round 1: 11 double crochet in the initial chain (12 double crochet made). Slip stitch in top of initial double crochet to join.

Round 2: Chain 3, double crochet in same st, 2 double crochet in every double crochet, slip stitch in top of initial double crochet to join. (24 double crochet)

Round 3: Chain 3, *chain 1, double crochet in subsequent double crochet, replicate from * all around ending with chain 1, slip stitch in top of initial double crochet to join.

Round 4: Chain 3, double crochet in same double crochet, *chain 2, 2double crochet-bobble in subsequent double crochet, replicate from * all around ending with chain 2, slip stitch in top of initial double crochet to join.

Round 5: *Chain 7, skip 1 bobble, single crochet in a subsequent bobble, replicate from * all around. (12 chain-7 loops made)

Round 6: Slip stitch to the corner of chain-7 loop, chain 3 (consider as 1 double crochet), 6 double crochet in the loop, *chain 2, 7 double crochet in the subsequent loop, replicate from * all around, ending with chain 2, slip stitch in initial double crochet to join.

Round 7: Chain 3, double crochet in subsequent 6 double crochet, *chain 2, double crochet in subsequent 7 double crochet, skip 2-chain space, double crochet in subsequent 7 double crochet, replicate from * all around ending with slip stitch in initial double crochet to join.

Round 8: Slip stitch to top of 2nd double crochet, chain 3, double crochet in subsequent 5 double crochet, *chain 3, double crochet in subsequent 6 double crochet, skip 2 double crochet, double crochet in subsequent 6 double crochet, replicate from * all around ending with slip stitch in initial double crochet to join.

Round 9: Slip stitch to top of 2nd double crochet, chain 3, double crochet in subsequent 4 double crochet, *chain 3, 5 double crochet in chain-3 space, chain 3, double crochet in subsequent 5 double crochet, skip 2 double crochet, double crochet in subsequent 5 double crochet, replicate from * all around, ending with slip stitch in initial double crochet to join.

Round 10: Slip stitch to top of 2nd double crochet, chain 3, double crochet in subsequent 3 double crochet, *chain 3, [double crochet in subsequent double crochet, chain 1] 4 times, double crochet in subsequent double crochet, chain 3, double crochet in subsequent 4 double crochet, skip 2 double crochet, double crochet in subsequent 4 double crochet, replicate from * all around, ending with slip stitch in initial double crochet to join.

Round 11: Slip stitch to top of 2nd double crochet, chain 3, double crochet in subsequent 2 double crochet, *chain 3, skip chain-3 space[single crochet in chain-1 loop, chain 3] 3 times, single crochet in last chain-1 loop, chain 3, double crochet in subsequent 3 double crochet, skip 2 double crochet, double crochet in subsequent 3 double crochet, replicate from * all around, ending with slip stitch in initial double crochet to join.

Round 12: Slip stitch to top of 2nd double crochet, chain 3, double crochet in subsequent double crochet, *chain 3, skip chain-3 space, [single crochet in chain-3 loop, chain 3] 2 times, single crochet in last chain-3 loop, chain 3, double crochet in subsequent 2 double crochet, skip 2 double crochet, double crochet in subsequent 2 double crochet, replicate from * all around, ending with slip stitch in initial double crochet to join.

Round 13: Chain 3, double crochet in subsequent double crochet, *chain 3, skip chain-3 space, single crochet in chain-3 loop, chain 3, single crochet in subsequent chain-3 loop, chain 3, double crochet2tog in subsequent 2 double crochet, chain 5, double crochet2tog in subsequent 2 double crochet, replicate from * all around, ending with chain 5, slip stitch in top of initial double crochet to join.

Round 14: Chain 6 (make 1 double crochet, chain 3), *skip chain-3 space, single crochet in chain-3 loop, chain 3, 7 double crochet in the chain-5 loop, chain 3, replicate from * all around ending with 6 double crochet in last chain-5 loop. Slip stitch in top of double crochet (3rd chain of chain 6) to join.

Round 15: Chain 6 (make 1 double crochet, chain 3), *skip (3 chain, single crochet, 3 chain), double crochet in subsequent double crochet, [chain 1, double crochet in subsequent double crochet] 6 times, chain 3, replicate from * all around ending with chain 1, slip stitch in top of initial double crochet to join.

Round 16: Slip stitch to chain-1 space, *chain 3, double crochet in chain-3 space, [chain 3, single crochet in chain-1 space] 6 times, replicate from * all around.

Round 17: Slip stitch up chain 3 to tip of double crochet, chain 3, 2 double crochet in same double crochet, *[chain 3, single crochet in chain-3 loop] 5 times, chain 3, 3 double crochet in subsequent double crochet, replicate from * all around ending with chain 3, slip stitch in initial double crochet to join.

Round 18: Chain 4 (consider as 1 double crochet, chain 1), double crochet in subsequent double crochet, chain 1, double crochet in subsequent double crochet, *[chain 3, single crochet in chain-3 loop] 4 times, chain 3, [double crochet in subsequent double crochet, chain 1] 2 times, double crochet in subsequent double crochet, replicate from * all around ending with chain 3, slip stitch in initial double crochet in to join.

Round 19: Chain 3, double crochet in same double crochet, *[chain 1, 2 double crochet in subsequent double crochet] 2 times, [chain 3, single crochet in chain-3 loop] 3 times, chain 3, 2 double crochet in subsequent double crochet, replicate from * all around, ending with chain 3, slip stitch in initial double crochet to join.

Round 20: Chain 3, double crochet in same double crochet, *[chain 1, 2 double crochet in subsequent double crochet] 5 times, [chain 3, single crochet in chain-3 loop] 2 times, chain 3, 2 double crochet in subsequent double crochet, replicate from * all around, ending with chain 3, slip stitch in initial double crochet to join. (You should have 12 2-double crochet groups in every single each scallop)

Round 21: Chain 3, double crochet in subsequent double crochet, *[chain 3, slip stitch in 3rd chain from hook to make picot, double crochet2tog in subsequent 2 double crochet] 5 times, chain 3, single crochet in chain-3 loop, picot, chain 3, double crochet2tog in subsequent 2 double crochet, replicate from * all around, ending with chain 3, slip stitch in initial double crochet to join. Tie up.

Dry and block. Use lace ribbon to weave 14 round and keep ribbon behind 7 (dc) double crochet group. Tie all ends of lace ribbon and make a knot as per your desire.

Pattern 10: Draw String Crochet Bag

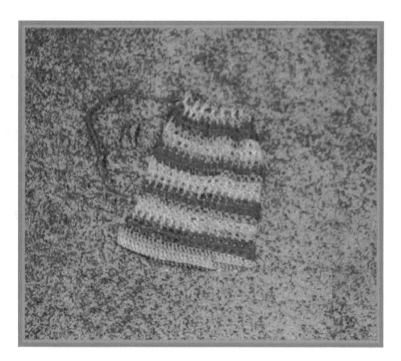

Crochet Hook: 5mm or H/8

Weight of Yarn: Aran and Wrosted/Medium Yarn (16 to 20 stitches to four inches)

Final Size: 12" long and 18" Around

Cotton Yarn: 129 yds or 3 oz.

Directions:

R: 1 - chain 34, 1 double crochet in the 4th chain from the hook, 1double crochet in the same chain as 1st double crochet,

1 double crochet in the following 29 chains, 2 double crochet in the last chain (33double crochet)

Turn working down the opposite side of the chain, 2 double crochet in the 1st chain,

1double crochet in the following 29 chains, 2 double crochet in the last chain, join to top of the 1st double crochet with a slip stitch,

(33double crochet + 33double crochet = 66double crochet)

R: 2 - chain3, (considers as a double crochet) 1 double crochet in every double crochet around, join, (66double crochet)

R: 3 -chain4, (considers as double crochet, chain1) *skip the following double crochet, 1 double crochet in the following double crochet, chain1*

Replicate from * to * around, join to top of chain 3 with a slip stitch, (33double crochet= 33chain1=66sts)

R: 4 - chain4, (considers as double crochet, chain1) *skip the following chain1 space, 1 double crochet in the following double crochet, chain1*

Replicate from * to * around, join to top of chain 3 with a slip stitch, (33double crochet= 33chain1=66sts)

R: 5 - R: 21 - Replicate R: 4

R: 6 - chain2, *1 half-double-crochet in the following double crochet, 1half-doublt-crochet in the following chain1 space*

Replicate from * to * around, join to 1st half-double-crochet with a slip stitch.

tie off and weave in your ends. (66half-doublt-crochet)

Drawstring:

using two strands of your cotton yarn, chain 100, tie up.

Weave ends of chain through Row 21

You can draw the drawstring to 1 side, for 1 side handle.

Or you can draw both ends, for two side handles.

Conclusion

Crafting can be really soothing for those people who are suffering from Dementia. Insomnia is a horrible feeling, but with the help of crocheting, you can get rid of this problem. Focus on soft and easy crochet and your mind and body will be relaxed to get to your bed. You can improve the quality of your sleep and reduce the need for sleep medications. This book is designed for you with 10 pretty crochet bag patterns. You can practice these patterns and improve your overall health. By selling these patterns, you can strengthen your financial position.

Crochet Book Covers
15 Wonderful Crochet Patterns To Cover Your Books

Introduction

Summer is drawing to a close, and with it our minds all turn back to books in one way or another. Perhaps you are a college student, and you are making ready to head off to school for the first time, the second time, or maybe it's even the last time.

Maybe you are entering high school, or maybe you are nearly finished. Maybe you are just happy to see all of the academic things come back into the picture, and you are getting your old books back off the shelves and enjoying them as you once did.

Perhaps you are ready to pick up book reading for the first time, and you are eager to start your very own personal library, getting only the books you want and the perfect personal touch added to each and every book you put onto your shelves.

No matter what you want to do, you have a good reason to get out your yarn, your crochet hook, and your favorite cup of coffee and get down to business. You are going to be able to add your own personal touch to each and every one of the titles.

Whether you are using soft cover, hard cover, repairing a cover that has long since seen better days, or simply redoing the cover to make it your own, you are going to find what you need in this book.

" I have never made a crochet cover before … is it hard? "

" I like to add my own touch to things, but I don't know how to make covers. "

" I don't want it to look like I did it wrong, or like I didn't know what I was doing. "

If you have ever felt any of these things, you aren't alone. Though making your own projects is exciting, it can be intimidating. But, you have everything you need right here to make your book a success, and it is going to give you the freedom you need to make your own covers any time you want, for any book you want.

And it just doesn ' t get any better than that.

Chapter 1 – The Basics

Zig Zag Zipper

You will need one ball of each color. I also use buttons for a clasp and a size G crochet hook.

Measure the length you need around the base of the book. If you are going to fold in the ends for the flap, add 6 inches onto this measurement.

Chain a length that is equal to this measurement, turn, and single crochet across the row.

For the next row, single crochet in the first 4 stitches, then skip the next stitch. Single crochet in the next 4 stitches, then skip the next stitch.

Continue to do this across the row, forming that zig zag pattern. Switch to the different color on the third row, and continue this pattern.

You will keep going now, switching up colors every third row until the cover fits over the cover of your book.

Tie it off when you have the right size, and chain a length of 15 for the closing band.

You are now ready to assemble.

To assemble:

You have more than one option when you assemble this cover ... either you can sew in panels to hold the book in place, or you can crochet an extra length and fold it over.

However you decide to do it, you are going to line up the ends, and sew the top and bottom of this row in place.

Attach the strap and the buttons, tie off and trim the loose threads, and your book is ready to slip inside!

Owl's Eyes Cover

You will need one ball of each color. I also use buttons for a clasp and a size G crochet hook.

Measure the length you need around the base of the book. If you are going to fold in the ends for the flap, add 6 inches onto this measurement.

Chain a length that is equal to this measurement, turn, and single crochet across the row.

For the next row, chain 1, and single crochet across the row. Chain 1, and single crochet back across the row.

Work until your cover is the size you need it to be. Measure as you go to ensure the proper fit, and tie off the end when you are finished.

For the eyes: Make 2

Start with black, and chain 5. Join with a slip stitch to form a ring.

Single crochet in the center of this 12 times. Change colors now to brown.

Work 1 row of brown before switching to white, and work 4 rows of white. Tie off and place on the cover as you see in the photo.

To assemble:

You have more than one option when you assemble this cover ... either you can sew in panels to hold the book in place, or you can crochet an extra length and fold it over.

However you decide to do it, you are going to line up the ends, and sew the top and bottom of this row in place.

Attach the strap and the buttons, tie off and trim the loose threads, and your book is ready to slip inside!

Blue And Gold Besties

You will need one ball of each color. I also use buttons for a clasp and a size G crochet hook.

Measure the length you need around the base of the book. If you are going to fold in the ends for the flap, add 6 inches onto this measurement.

Chain a length that is equal to this measurement, turn, and single crochet across the row.

For the next row, chain 2, and double crochet across the row. Chain 2, and double crochet back across the row.

Work until your cover is the size you need it to be. Measure as you go to ensure the proper fit, and tie off the end when you are finished with this section.

To assemble:

You have more than one option when you assemble this cover … either you can sew in panels to hold the book in place, or you can crochet an extra length and fold it over.

However you decide to do it, you are going to line up the ends, and sew the top and bottom of this row in place.

Attach the strap and the buttons, tie off and trim the loose threads, and your book is ready to slip inside!

Chapter 2 – Cute As a Button

Christmas Crashes

You will need one ball of each color. I also use buttons for a clasp and a size G crochet hook.

Measure the length you need around the base of the book. If you are going to fold in the ends for the flap, add 6 inches onto this measurement.

This is the total length you need your book cover to be, but you are going to start by chaining a length that is equal to the height of the book.

Single crochet across the row.

For the next row, chain 1, and single crochet back across the row. Chain 1, and single crochet across the row.

For the next row, you are going to work a single crochet row, working in the front row only.

Continue to single crochet back and forth across the row, every third row you are going to use the same single crochet, but you are going to only do it in the front loop only. Continue until it is the length you need.

To assemble:

You have more than one option when you assemble this cover ... either you can sew in panels to hold the book in place, or you can crochet an extra length and fold it over.

However you decide to do it, you are going to line up the ends, and sew the top and bottom of this row in place.

Attach the strap and the buttons, tie off and trim the loose threads, and your book is ready to slip inside!

Green Striped Goodness

You will need one ball of each color. I also use buttons for a clasp and a size G crochet hook.

Measure the length you need around the base of the book. If you are going to fold in the ends for the flap, add 6 inches onto this measurement.

Chain a length that is equal to this measurement, turn, and single crochet across the row.

For the next row, chain 2, and double crochet across the row. Chain 2, and double crochet back across the row.

You are going to change colors every other row, so keep an eye on the photo to see when you change colors.

For the strap, you are going to chain 5, and single crochet across the row until it is long enough to close the book you want to cover.

For the flower:

Chain 5. Join with a slip stitch to form a ring.

Single crochet in the center of this 12 times. Join with a slip stitch, and chain 1. Single crochet in the next stitch 3 times, and single crochet in the next stitch. Single crochet in the next stitch 3 times, and single crochet in the next stitch.

Repeat around, and tie off.

To assemble:

You have more than one option when you assemble this cover … either you can sew in panels to hold the book in place, or you can crochet an extra length and fold it over.

However you decide to do it, you are going to line up the ends, and sew the top and bottom of this row in place.

Attach the strap and the buttons, tie off and trim the loose threads, and your book is ready to slip inside!

Meadow Madness

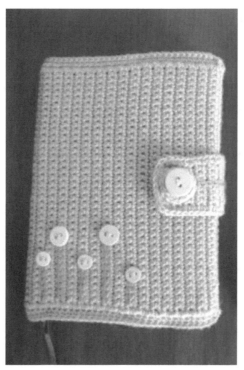

You will need one ball of each color. I also use buttons for a clasp and a size G crochet hook.

Measure the length you need around the base of the book. If you are going to fold in the ends for the flap, add 6 inches onto this measurement.

This is the total length you need your book cover to be, but you are going to start by chaining a length that is equal to the height of the book.

Single crochet across the row.

For the next row, chain 1, and single crochet back across the row. Chain 1, and single crochet across the row. Continue to single crochet back and forth across the row until it is the length you need.

Work 1 row of single crochet for the boarder.

For the strap, you are going to chain 5, and single crochet across the row until it is long enough to close the book you want to cover.

To assemble:

You have more than one option when you assemble this cover … either you can sew in panels to hold the book in place, or you can crochet an extra length and fold it over.

However you decide to do it, you are going to line up the ends, and sew the top and bottom of this row in place.

You are going to add in the details with a sewing needle, thread, and a yarn needle. Attach the decorations as you see in the photo.

Attach the strap and the buttons, tie off and trim the loose threads, and your book is ready to slip inside!

Chapter 3 – Just What You Wanted

Handy Handle

You will need one ball of each color. I also use buttons for a clasp and a size G crochet hook.

Measure the length you need around the base of the book. If you are going to fold in the ends for the flap, add 6 inches onto this measurement.

Chain a length that is equal to this measurement, turn, and single crochet across the row.

For the next row, single crochet across the row. Chain 1, turn, and single crochet back across the other way. Continue to do this until you have the right size, and tie off.

For the handle:

Measure the overall length you need for the book, and chain a length that is equal to this, plus 8 inches.

Work a single crochet pattern for the next 8 rows, and tie off.

Watch the photo for placement of the strap, and sew in place accordingly.

To assemble:

You have more than one option when you assemble this cover ... either you can sew in panels to hold the book in place, or you can crochet an extra length and fold it over.

However you decide to do it, you are going to line up the ends, and sew the top and bottom of this row in place.

Attach the strap and the buttons, tie off and trim the loose threads, and your book is ready to slip inside!

The Lady of Lace

You will need one ball of each color. I also use buttons for a clasp and a size G crochet hook.

Measure the length you need around the base of the book. If you are going to fold in the ends for the flap, add 6 inches onto this measurement.

Chain a length that is equal to this measurement, turn, and single crochet across the row.

For the next row, single crochet across the row. Chain 1, turn, and single crochet back across the other way. Continue to do this until you have the right size, and tie off.

Now, repeat these steps once more, only this time with the other color. You are going to use your yarn needle to sew these two pieces in place, and tie off.

To assemble:

You have more than one option when you assemble this cover … either you can sew in panels to hold the book in place, or you can crochet an extra length and fold it over.

However you decide to do it, you are going to line up the ends, and sew the top and bottom of this row in place.

Attach the strap and the buttons, tie off and trim the loose threads, and your book is ready to slip inside!

Crazy Days

You will need one ball of each color. I also use buttons for a clasp and a size G crochet hook.

Measure the length you need around the base of the book. If you are going to fold in the ends for the flap, add 6 inches onto this measurement.

This is the total length you need your book cover to be, but you are going to start by chaining a length that is equal to the height of the book.

Single crochet across the row.

For the next row, chain 1, and single crochet back across the row. Chain 1, and single crochet across the row. Continue to single crochet back and forth across the row until it is the length you need.

To assemble:

You have more than one option when you assemble this cover … either you can sew in panels to hold the book in place, or you can crochet an extra length and fold it over.

However you decide to do it, you are going to line up the ends, and sew the top and bottom of this row in place.

Attach the strap and the buttons, tie off and trim the loose threads, and your book is ready to slip inside!

Chapter 4 – Books and Books

Multi-Goodness Goddess

You will need one ball of each color. I also use buttons for a clasp and a size G crochet hook.

Measure the length you need around the base of the book. If you are going to fold in the ends for the flap, add 6 inches onto this measurement.

Chain a length that is equal to this measurement, turn, and single crochet across the row.

For the next row, chain 1, and single crochet back across the row. Chain 1, and single crochet across the row. Continue to single crochet back and forth across the row until it is the length you need.

To assemble:

You have more than one option when you assemble this cover ... either you can sew in panels to hold the book in place, or you can crochet an extra length and fold it over.

However you decide to do it, you are going to line up the ends, and sew the top and bottom of this row in place.

Attach the strap and the buttons, tie off and trim the loose threads, and your book is ready to slip inside!

Pleased as a Plum

You will need one ball of each color. I also use buttons for a clasp and a size G crochet hook.

Measure the length you need around the base of the book. If you are going to fold in the ends for the flap, add 6 inches onto this measurement.

Chain a length that is equal to this measurement, turn, and single crochet across the row.

For the next row, chain 2, and double crochet back across the row. Chain 2, and double crochet across the row. Continue to single crochet back and forth across the row until it is the length you need.

Work 1 row of single crochet on the boarder, and repeat the main sequence for the strap.

For the flower:

Chain 5. Join with a slip stitch to form a ring.

Single crochet in the center of this 12 times. Join with a slip stitch, and chain 1. Single crochet in the next stitch 3 times, and single crochet in the next stitch. Single crochet in the next stitch 3 times, and single crochet in the next stitch.

Repeat around, and tie off.

To assemble:

You have more than one option when you assemble this cover … either you can sew in panels to hold the book in place, or you can crochet an extra length and fold it over.

However you decide to do it, you are going to line up the ends, and sew the top and bottom of this row in place.

Attach the strap and the buttons, tie off and trim the loose threads, and your book is ready to slip inside!

Green Machine

You will need one ball of each color. I also use buttons for a clasp and a size G crochet hook.

Measure the length you need around the base of the book. If you are going to fold in the ends for the flap, add 6 inches onto this measurement.

This is the total length you need your book cover to be, but you are going to start by chaining a length that is equal to the height of the book.

Single crochet across the row.

For the next row, chain 1, and single crochet back across the row. Chain 1, and single crochet across the row. Continue to single crochet back and forth across the row until it is the length you need.

You are now going to decrease with each row, skipping the first 2 stitches on each row, and stopping 2 stitches before the end of each row. When you are at a fine point, tie it off.

You are now ready to assemble.

To assemble:

You have more than one option when you assemble this cover ... either you can sew in panels to hold the book in place, or you can crochet an extra length and fold it over.

However you decide to do it, you are going to line up the ends, and sew the top and bottom of this row in place.

Attach the strap and the buttons, tie off and trim the loose threads, and your book is ready to slip inside!

Chapter 5 – The Best of the Rest

The Pretty Pastel

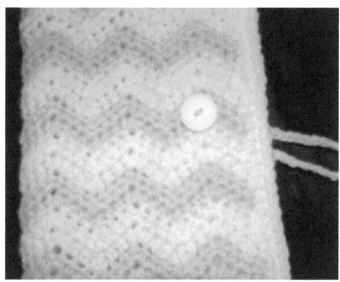

You will need one ball of each color. I also use buttons for a clasp and a size G crochet hook.

Measure the length you need around the base of the book. If you are going to fold in the ends for the flap, add 6 inches onto this measurement.

Chain a length that is equal to this measurement, turn, and single crochet across the row.

For the next row, single crochet in the first 4 stitches, then skip the next stitch. Single crochet in the next 4 stitches, then skip the next stitch.

Continue to do this across the row, forming that zig zag pattern. Switch to the different color on the third row, and continue this pattern.

You will keep going now, switching up colors every third row until the cover fits over the cover of your book.

Tie it off when you have the right size, and chain two lengths of 10 for the ties.

You are now ready to assemble.

To assemble:

You have more than one option when you assemble this cover ... either you can sew in panels to hold the book in place, or you can crochet an extra length and fold it over.

However you decide to do it, you are going to line up the ends, and sew the top and bottom of this row in place.

Attach the strap and the buttons, tie off and trim the loose threads, and your book is ready to slip inside!

Rainbow Valley Beauty Book

You will need one ball of each color. I also use buttons for a clasp and a size G crochet hook.

Measure the length you need around the base of the book. If you are going to fold in the ends for the flap, add 6 inches onto this measurement.

This is the total length you need your book cover to be, but you are going to start by chaining a length that is equal to the height of the book.

Single crochet across the row.

For the next row, chain 1, and single crochet back across the row. Chain 1, and single crochet across the row. Continue to single crochet back and forth across the row until it is the length you need.

For the strap:

You are going to start with a chain 5 stitches long.

Continue to work until you are happy with the size of the length, and single crochet a boarder around the entire strap.

To assemble:

You have more than one option when you assemble this cover … either you can sew in panels to hold the book in place, or you can crochet an extra length and fold it over.

However you decide to do it, you are going to line up the ends, and sew the top and bottom of this row in place.

Attach the strap and the buttons, tie off and trim the loose threads, and your book is ready to slip inside!

The Scholar Cover

You will need one ball of each color. I also use buttons for a clasp and a size G crochet hook.

Measure the length you need around the base of the book. If you are going to fold in the ends for the flap, add 6 inches onto this measurement.

Chain a length that is equal to this measurement, turn, and single crochet across the row.

For the next row, single crochet across the row. Chain 1, turn, and single crochet back across the other way. Continue to do this until you have the right size, and tie off.

To assemble:

You have more than one option when you assemble this cover … either you can sew in panels to hold the book in place, or you can crochet an extra length and fold it over.

However you decide to do it, you are going to line up the ends, and sew the top and bottom of this row in place.

Attach the strap and the buttons, tie off and trim the loose threads, and your book is ready to slip inside!

Chapter 6 – Making It Your Own

You will see that there are a lot of different ways you can make the covers for your books, you are going to find the same general pattern for each book. Since books are generally the same shape, you are going to use the same overall shape for each of your covers.

But, you don't have to stop there.

As you can see from the patterns in this book, you can add your own little touches here and there, but there is so much more you can do than just add a flower here or a strap there.

Every time you finish a cover, take a look at it and decide what you want to do with it.

You will find all kinds of patches, stamps, material, stickers, and tons of other options to use for each and every cover. Go to your local craft store and look over all of the various options you can choose from to customize your cover.

Add a different piece to each cover you make, and mix and match to create something entirely new each time. When you are being creative, there is no way you can go wrong. If you want to make a thicker strap, do it. If you want to have a thinner strap, or no strap at all, then you have the complete freedom to do that.

The main thing you want to keep in mind is that this should be fun. Add colors, add buttons, add anything you want. Make each and every book cover able to zip, or make them as open as the book itself.

In other words, treat each project as entirely unique and its own creation. You are going to be able to change and modify each and every one of these patterns to be just what you want them to be, or you can make each and every one as much the same as each other as you can.

The biggest benefit that comes from creating your own cover is that you have the freedom to make it your own.

So go ahead.

Make them your own.

Conclusion

There you have it, everything you need to know to completely make over your book collection, and to add your own personal taste to anything and everything you want in the book world.

You really don't need to have a reason to makeover your book collection, and the more you do it, the more you are going to find to do. I hope this book was able to inspire you to engage your other books, no matter how you want to do that.

I want you to have fun with the best collection you can ever have in life ... your books. I want them to look like you want them to look, to give them your added touch of character. I want you to fall in love with your books for a whole new reason, and I want you to keep coming back to them over and over again.

This book is designed to help you make friends of your other books, and to fall in love with them, to give them your own little spin in any way you can think of. You don't have to be an author to make your mark on a book, and you don't need to be an artist to make your own book covers.

With this book, you are given everything you need to make your mark on any book, or even a tablet or computer if you want to. There's no way you can go wrong with your own creativity, and this book wants to give you everything you need to get started with your own personal library.

All you need is a few dollar's worth of supplies, a few minutes of your time, and a little bit of inspiration, and you have everything you need to get your project up and running. So if you are ready to say hello to the joys of making your own book covers, you have come to the right place.

Cover each and every book you own, buy more books to cover, and cover all your friends' books. No matter how you want to go about it, you are free to do as you please.

Let your creativity shine, and embrace your unique self. No matter how you want to do it, you are going to have it your way.

Crochet Mandala:
12 Most Gorgeous Patterns With Easy Instructions

Introduction

Crochet craft is beneficial for everyone because it can improve your overall health and decrease your stress and tensions. You can learn the basic stitches of crochet to prepare these patterns easily. Crochet craft can fill your pocket with money because you can sell them in the market physically or via online stores. In this book, there are 12 beautiful mandala patterns with easy instructions. Follow them to design your own 12 mandalas.

Chapter 1 – 12 Most Gorgeous Patterns With Easy Instructions

These 12 patterns are easy to follow and perfect for you to decorate your house or send as gift to your friends:

Pattern 01: Blooming Mandala

Crochet Hook: 5mm or H/8

Weight of Yarn: (4) Aran and Worsted/Medium Weight (16 to 20 stitches to four inches)

Final Size: 12.5 to 13.5 inches

Notes:

- You will work in rounds with sl st (slip stitch) in the first stitch from the final stitch.
- You should learn to create slip knot on your hook.
- In some rows, the chain 1 will not be taken as a stitch.
- You will use nine colors in this pattern, and you are free to reduce them or use them all. You can repeat a few colors.
- Block the finish items and wet block can be a good choice for this.
- There is no need to fasten off any color until you are satisfied with the row.

- Monitor your stitches with any stitch counter.

Description:

Round 1: Color 1: Create a magic circle, ch 1, single crochet six times into the circle, slip stitch into the first st to secure – 6 single crochets

Round 2: Ch 7 (counts as treble + 3), *treble into the subsequent st, ch 3,* replicate from * to * 4 more times, slip stitch into the top of the ch 4 to secure – 6 trebles, six ch-3 spaces

Fasten off Color 1.

Round 3: Color 2: Create a slip knot on your hook, single crochet into a ch-3 space, single crochet 3 more times into the similar ch-3 space, ch 1, skip the subsequent treble, *single crochet 4 times into the following ch-3 space, ch 1, skip the subsequent treble,* replicate from * to * 4 more times, slip stitch into the first st to secure – 24 single crochets, 6 ch-1 spaces

Round 4: Ch 2 (counts as the first leg of the double-crochet4together), double-crochet3together the subsequent 3 sts, skip the subsequent ch 1 space, ch 8, *double-crochet4together the subsequent 4 sts, skip the subsequent ch 1 space, ch 8,* replicate from * to * 4 more times, slip stitch into the top of the double-crochet3together to secure – 6 double-crochet4togethers, 6 ch-8 spaces

Fasten off Color 2.

Round 5: 3rd color: Create a slip knot on your hook, single crochet 4 times into a ch-8 space, double-treble into the ch-1 space from round 2, single crochet 4 times into the similar ch-8 space, ch 3, skip the subsequent double-crochet4together, *[single crochet 4 times, double-treble (double-treble) into the ch-1 space from round 2, single crochet 4 times] into the subsequent ch-8 space, ch 3, skip the later double-crochet4together,* replicate from * to * 4 more times, slip stitch into the first st to secure – 48 single crochets, 6 double-treble, 6 ch-3 spaces

Fasten off 3rd color.

Round 6: 4th color: Ch 1, single crochet into the similar st as join, single crochet into the subsequent 8 sts (this includes both single crochet and double-treble), [2 single crochet, picot, 2 single crochet] into the following ch-3 space, *single crochet into the subsequent 9 sts, [2 single crochet, picot, 2 single crochet] into the subsequent ch-3 space,* replicate from * to * 4 more times, slip stitch into the first st to secure – 78 single crochets, 6 picots

Tie-up 4th color.

Round 7: 5th Color: Create a slip knot on your hook, spike single crochet around the first single crochet of the subsequent [2 single crochet, picot, 2 single crochet] in a ch-3 space, ch 10, spike single crochet around the last single crochet of the similar [2 single crochet, picot, 2 single crochet], ch 20, *spike single crochet spike single crochet around the first single crochet of the subsequent [2 single crochet, picot, 2 single crochet] in a ch-3 space, ch 10, spike single crochet around the last single crochet of the similar [2 single crochet, picot, 2 single crochet], ch 20,* replicate from * to * 4 more times, slip stitch into the first spike single crochet to secure – 12 spike single crochets, 6 ch-10 spaces, 6 ch-20 spaces

Tie up 5th color.

Round 8: 6th color: Create a slip knot on your hook, single crochet into a ch 20 space, single crochet 4 more times, ch 15, skip the subsequent [spike single crochet, ch-10, spike single crochet], *single crochet 5 times into the subsequent ch-20 space, ch 15, skip the subsequent [spike single crochet, ch-10, spike single crochet],*replicate from * to * 4 more times, slip stitch into the first st to secure – 30 single crochets, 6 ch-15 spaces

Round 9: Ch 1, single crochet into the similar st as join, single crochet into the subsequent st, picot, skip the subsequent st, single crochet into the subsequent 2 stitches, front post SeptTreble around the subsequent double-treble from round 5, [10 half-double-crochet, ch 5, 10 half-double-crochet] into the subsequent ch-20 space, *single crochet into the subsequent 2 sts, picot, skip the subsequent st, single crochet into the subsequent 2 sts, front post SeptTreble around the subsequent double-treble from round 5, [10 half-double-crochet, ch 5, 10 half-double-crochet] into the subsequent ch-20 space,* replicate from * to * 4 more times, slip stitch into the first st to secure – 24 single crochets, 6 picots, 6 ch-5 spaces, 6 SeptTrebles (septule-treble-crochet), 120 half-double-crochets

Tie up 6th color.

Round 10: 7th color: Pull up a loop in the first single crochet of a [2 single crochet, picot, 2 single crochet] section, ch 7 (counts as a treble and a ch 3 space), skip the subsequent [single crochet, picot, single crochet], treble into the subsequent st, ch 2, omit the subsequent 4 sts, half-double-crochet into the subsequent 5 sts, skip the subsequent 2 sts, half-double-crochet 6 times into the subsequent ch-5 space, skip the subsequent 2 sts, half-double-crochet into the subsequent 5 sts, ch 2, skip the subsequent 3 sts, *treble into the subsequent single crochet, ch 3, skip the subsequent [single crochet, picot, single crochet], treble into the subsequent st, ch 2, skip the subsequent 4 sts, half-double-crochet into the subsequent 5 sts, skip the subsequent 2 sts, half-double-crochet 6 times into the subsequent ch-5 space, skip the subsequent 2 sts, half-double-crochet into the subsequent 5 sts, ch 2, skip the subsequent 3 sts,* replicate from * to * 4 more times, slip stitch into the 4th st from the bottom of the original ch-7 to secure – 12 trebles, 96 half-double-crochets, 6 ch-3 spaces, 12 ch-2 spaces

Tie up the 7th color.

Round 11: 8th color: Create a slip knot on your hook, single crochet into a ch-3 space, ch 5, skip the subsequent [treble, ch-2 space, half-double-crochet], half-double-crochet into the subsequent 2 sts, SeptTreble into the ch-10 space from round 7 (skip the corresponding st on the round here and throughout this round), half-double-crochet into the subsequent st, ch 3, skip the subsequent 2 sts, single crochet into the subsequent st, ch 3, single crochet into the subsequent st, ch 3, skip the subsequent 2 sts, half-double-crochet into the subsequent St, SeptTreble into the ch-10 space from round 7, half-double-crochet into the subsequent 2 sts, ch 5, skip the subsequent [half-double-crochet, ch-2, treble], single crochet into the subsequent ch-3 space, ch 5, skip the subsequent [treble, ch-2 space, half-double-crochet], half-double-crochet into the subsequent 2 sts, SeptTreble into the ch-10 space from round 7 (skip the corresponding st on the round here and throughout this round), half-double-crochet into the subsequent st, ch 3, skip the subsequent 2 sts, single crochet into the subsequent st, ch 3, single crochet into the subsequent st, ch 3, skip the subsequent 2 sts, half-double-crochet into the subsequent st, SeptTreble into the ch-10 space from round 7, half-double-crochet into the subsequent 2 sts, ch 5, skip the subsequent [half-double-crochet, ch-2, treble],* replicate from * to * 4 more times, slip stitch into the first st to secure – 18 single crochets, 12 ch-5 spaces, 36 half-double-crochets, 12 SeptTrebles, 18 ch-3 spaces.

Tie up the 8th color.

Round 12: 9th color: Pull up a loop in the ch-5 space left of the first single crochet of the previous round, ch 4 (counts as a treble), [treble, Ch 3, 2 treble] into the similar ch 5 space, ch 2, skip the subsequent half-double-crochet, half-double-crochet into the subsequent 3 sts, double-crochet 3 times into the subsequent ch-3 space, ch 2, skip the subsequent single crochet, double-crochet 7 times into the subsequent ch-3 space, ch 2, skip the subsequent single crochet, double-crochet 3 times into the subsequent ch-3 space, half-double-crochet in the subsequent 3 sts, ch 2, skip the subsequent half-double-crochet, [2 treble, ch 3, 2 treble] into the subsequent ch-5 space, ch 2, skip the subsequent single crochet, *[2 treble, ch 3, 2 treble] into the subsequent ch-5 space, ch 2, skip the subsequent half-double-crochet, half-double-crochet into the subsequent 3 sts, double-crochet 3 times into the subsequent ch-3 space, ch 2, skip the subsequent single crochet, double-crochet 7 times into the subsequent ch-3 space, ch 2, skip the subsequent single crochet, double-crochet 3 times into the subsequent ch-3 space, half-double-crochet in the subsequent 3 sts, ch 2, skip the subsequent half-double-crochet, [2 treble, ch 3, 2 treble] into the subsequent ch-5 space, ch 2, skip the subsequent single crochet,* replicate from * to * 4 more times, slip stitch into the top of the original ch-4 to secure -48 trebles, 12 ch-3 spaces, 30 ch-2 spaces, 18 half-double-crochets, 78 double-crochets

Tie-up 9th color.

Carefully weave all ends.

Pattern 02: Flower Madala

Crochet Hook: 6.5mm or K/10.5

Weight of Yarn: Bulky Yarn (5) (12 to 15 stitches for four inches)

Round 1: With the first color, chain 2. Work 10 half-double-crochet in 2nd chain from hook. Join. (10 stitches)

Round 2: ch 1. Work 2 single crochet in each st around. Join. (20 stitches)

Round 3: chain 1. *Work 3 double crochet in subsequent st. Skip 1 st*. Replicate (*) around. Join. (30 stitches, or ten "clusters")

Round 4: ch 1. Working between the clusters for this round, *double crochet, three treble crochet, double crochet*. Replicate (*) around. Join. (50 stitches)

Round 5: Slip stitches over to the 2nd treble crochet. Chain 1. Single crochet in top of center treble crochet. Chain 5. *Skip subsequent four stitches. Single crochet in top of subsequent center treble crochet. Ch 5*. Replicate (*) around. Join. (10 stitches + 10 chain 5 spaces)

Round 6: ch 1. *Single crochet in single crochet st. Work {2 double crochet, treble crochet, ch 1. slip stitch in top of treble crochet just worked, treble crochet, two double crochet} in subsequent chain five space*. Replicate (*) around. Join. Tie-up and weave all ends.

Pattern 03: *Mandala Beanie*

- **Crochet Hook: 3.5mm or E/4 along with 4mm or G/6 hook**
- **Weight of Yarn: (0) Lace (33 to 40 stitches to four inches)**
- **Color A: Blue**
- **Color B: Cerise**
- **Color C: Purple**
- **Color D: Orange**
- **Weaving Needle**

Directions:

You will work top-down, and the brim is attached to the hat after finishing its body. This hat may look like different, and its fitting will be irregular than ordinary hats.

Guage:

- Four Rounds: 2.25 inches crossways
- Nine Rounds: 7.25 inches crossways
- Fifteen Rounds: 10.25 inches crossways

Special Stitches

Bltr (Beginning-linked-treble-crochet): Skip initial chain (insert crochet hook in the subsequent chain, yarn over, pull loop through) three times, (yarn over, pull through two loops o crochet hook) three times.

Ltr (Linked-Treble-Crochet): (insert crochet hook in the horizontal bar on one side of the previous stitch, yarn over and pull the loop through) two times, insert crochet hook in the subsequent chain, yarn over, pull loop through, [yarn over, pull through two loops on crochet hook] three times.

Directions:

Rnd 1: Start working with a larger crochet hook and use thread A, chain 4, link with slip stitch to the first ch to form a ring, ch 1, eight single crochet in ring, slip stitch to first single crochet. (Stitch count: 8 single crochet) Rnd 2: Chain 1, two single crochet in every single crochet all the way around, slip stitch to first single crochet. (Stitch count: 16 single crochet) Rnd 3: Chain 1, [single crochet in single crochet, two single crochet in subsequent single crochet] all the way around. (Stitch count: 24 single crochet) Tie up A.

Rnd 4: Use B color, working in bl (back loops) only for this rnd, join with slip stitch in any single crochet, chain 3 (it is considered as double crochet), double crochet in same single crochet as joining, *double crochet in subsequent single crochet, 2 double crochet in following single crochet, replicate from * to last single crochet, double crochet in last single crochet, slip stitch to top of beg ch-3. (Stitch count: 36 double crochet) Tie-upB.

Rnd 5: Use Color C, join with slip stitch in any double crochet, *ch 12, bltr, ltr in every remaining ch, skip 2 double crochet from rnd 4, slip stitch to subsequent double crochet with D (9 ltr-petal made), drop color C, now start with D, replicate from *, changing to C on slip stitch, carry on replicate from * until 12 petals are created, alternating colors, ending with slip stitch in first slip stitch. Carefully change color to avoid "cupping" of the project. If you want this strand on the back, you can cut off every petal to change colors. Or, alternatively, work this rnd in only one color. (Stitch count: 12 9-ltr petals created) Tie-upC and D.

Rnd 6: With A, join with slip stitch to the bottom of any petal on the base row side (where you did your initial chain 12), chain 1, *9 single crochet along side of petal, [2 single crochet in unused loop of chain at top of petal] 2 times, 9 single crochet along opposite side of petal, ch 3, slip stitch in unused corresponding front loop of single crochet of rnd 3, ch 3, replicate from * all the way around every of 12 petals, slip stitch to first single crochet.

Rnd 7: Slip stitch to 5th single crochet at side of the petal, ch 1, *single crochet in subsequent six single crochet, chain 1, single crochet in subsequent six single crochet, skip ten single crochet, replicate from * until all petals completed, slip stitch to first single crochet.

Rnd 8: Ch 1, *single crochet in subsequent five single crochet, three single crochet in ch-1 sp, single crochet in subsequent five single crochet, skip two single crochet, replicate from * until all petals are completed, slip stitch to first single crochet.

Rnd 9: Slip stitch to subsequent single crochet, ch 1, *single crochet in subsequent 4 single crochet, 3 single crochet in subsequent single crochet, single crochet in subsequent 4 single crochet, ch 3, skip 4 single crochet, replicate from * until all petals completed, slip stitch to first single crochet. Tie-upA.

Rnd 10: Join B with slip stitch in any ch-3 sp, ch 4 (counts as tr here and throughout), 8 tr in same ch 3 sp, *single crochet in 2nd single crochet of 3-single crochet group at top of petal, 9 treble in subsequent ch-3 sp, replicate from *, ending with single crochet in last petal, slip stitch to top of beginning ch-4. Tie-upB.

Rnd 11: Join A with slip stitch in any single crochet, ch 4, 6 tr in same single crochet, *skip tr, single crochet in subsequent 7 tr, skip tr, 7 tr in single crochet at top of subsequent petal, replicate from * to last 9-tr group, skip tr, single crochet in subsequent 7 tr, skip tr, slip stitch to top of beginning ch-4.

Rnd 12: Ch 1, single crochet in the same tr as joining and in subsequent six tr, *hdouble crochet in subsequent seven single crochet, single crochet in subsequent seven tr, replicate from * ending with hdouble crochet in last 7 single crochet, slip stitch to first single crochet. Tie-upA.

Rnd 13: Working in bl (back loops) only for this rnd, join D with slip stitch in top of same beginning st of previous rnd, ch 3, skip joining St, double crochet in every st all the way around, slip stitch to top of beginning ch-3. (Stitch count: 168 double crochet) Tie-upD.

Rnd 14: Join A with slip stitch in top of same beginning ch-3, ch 1, single crochet in same joining st, single crochet in subsequent 2 double crochet, *double crochet in corresponding unworked front loop of st from rnd below (in this rnd, you're looking at the stitches in rnd 12), skip double crochet behind double crochet just worked, single crochet in subsequent 3 double crochet, replicate from * to last st, double crochet in corresponding unworked front loop of single crochet from rnd below, skip double crochet behind double crochet just worked, slip stitch to first single crochet.

Rnd 15: Ch 1, single crochet in every stitch all the way around, slip stitch to first single crochet. (stitch count: 168 single crochet) Tie up A.

Rnd 16: Working in bl (back loops) only for this rnd, join C with slip stitch in top of same single crochet as joining, ch 3, skip joining st, double crochet in every st all the way around, slip stitch to top of beginning ch-3, (stitch count: 168 double crochet) Tie-up C.

Rnds 17-18: With A, replicate rnds 14-15. Tie-up A.

Rnd 19: Working in bl (back loops) only for this rnd, join B with slip stitch in top of same single crochet as joining, ch 3, skip joining st, double crochet in every st all the way around, slip stitch to top of beginning ch-3, (stitch count: 168 double crochet) Tie-upB.

Rnds 20-21: With A, replicate rnds 14to 15. Tie-up A.

Rnd 22: Working in bl (back loops) only for this rnd, join D with slip stitch in top of same single crochet as joining, ch 3, skip joining st, double crochet in every st all the way around, slip stitch to top of beginning ch-3, (stitch count: 168 double crochet) Tie-upD.

Rnds 23-24: Replicate rnds 14-15. Do not Tie-up A.

Brim

Row 1: (Still attached to hat, ribbing is worked vertically along stitches of hat.) With smaller hook and A, ch 9, single crochet in the second ch from hook and in subsequent seven ch, on hat body skip two single crochet from rnd 24, slip stitch in subsequent st, turn ribbing.

Row 2: Working in bl (back loops) only, single crochet in 8 single crochet, turn ribbing.

Row 3: Ch 1, working in bl (back loops) only, single crochet in 8 single crochet, on hat body skip 2 single crochet from rnd 24, slip stitch in subsequent st, turn ribbing.

Replicate rows 2-3 until all stitches used from rnd 24, carefully fasten off.

Finishing

It is time to use your yarn needle and stitch the brim, securely weave all ends.

Pattern 04: Crochet Doily

Start your work with 12mm crochet hook and two skeins yarn.

R1: Ch8, slip stitch in the first chain to link a ring. Ch3, 17double crochet in ring. Slip stitch in top of beginning ch3. (18double crochet)

R2: Ch4, do not flip. (Double crochet in subsequent st, ch1) around. Join with slip stitch in 3rd ch of beginning ch4.

R3: Slip stitch in subsequent ch sp. Ch3, 2double crochet in the same sp. 3double crochet in each remaining ch sp. Join with slip stitch to beginning ch3. (54double crochet)

R4: Ch1. Work the following crossways ea 3double crochet group: Single crochet in 1st double crochet, half-double-crochet in 2nd double crochet, double crochet in 3rd double crochet, chain 3.

R5: Slip stitch in beginning single crochet made. Slip stitch in double crochet. Single crochet in the three ch space. Ch5 (Single crochet in the space between the subsequent double crochet and three chains, ch5) around. Slip stitch in beginning single crochet made.

R6: Ch5. (Single crochet in subsequent ch5 space, ch5) around. Instead of finishing with ch5, end with ch2 and double crochet in first single crochet.

R7: Ch1. In the subsequent loop: (Single crochet, ch5, single crochet) chain 1 and subsequent loop (single crochet, ch5, single crochet). Continue around, and after last single crochet ch1 and slip stitch in beginning single crochet.

R8: Slip stitch in the initial 5ch loop, single crochet into a loop, ch6, single crochet in the subsequent loop, ch6 around. After the last ch6, slip stitch into initial single crochet.

R9: Ch3, five double crochet in the loop, one double crochet in subsequent single crochet, five double crochet in the loop, one double crochet in following single crochet. Continue around, finishing with 6double crochet in the last loop, and join with slip stitch to top of initial ch3.

R10: Ch1, single crochet in the same stitch, half-double-crochet in subsequent stitch, double crochet in following stitch, chain 3. Continue with single crochet,half-double-crochet,double crochet,ch3 sequence around and join with slip stitch to the first stitch.

R11: Slip stitches up to 3 ch loops. Single crochet in the loop, ch5, single crochet in a subsequent loop. After last ch5 join with slip stitch to initial single crochet.

R12: Single crochet in the loop, chain 5, single crochet in the subsequent loop, ch5. Continue around, and at finish ch2 and double crochet in first single crochet.

R13: Ch3, three double crochet in initial ch5 loop, 4double crochet in the subsequent loop, and four double crochet in every ch5 loop around. Join to initial chain with slip stitch.

R 14 chain 1 *Sk 1 st, six double crochet in subsequent st, sk 1 st, single crochet in subsequent st* continue around and slip stitch at first ch.

R15 chain 5 (counts as one double crochet + chain 2), *single crochet in 4th double crochet, chain 2, double crochet in single crochet between shells, chain 2* continue around and slip stitch at 3rd ch of the initial five ch.

R 16 *Chain 3, sc subsequent ch2 sp, (double crochet,ch2, double crochet) in subsequent single crochet (V-st made), ch3, sk following ch2 sp, slip stitch in subsequent six stitches, repeat from * continue around and slip stitch in initial st.

R 17 ch1, Sk subsequent ch2 sp of round 16, *5double crochet in each of following three ch3 spaces (fan made), sk subsequent three slip stitch single crochet in following slip stitch (above single crochet from round 15); repeat from * around, slip stitch in beginning ch to join.

R18: Optional. Single crochet around, for pointing, crochet 3double crochet in the middle double crochet in each of the fan. Tie up and weave in the end.

Pattern 05: Spring Rug

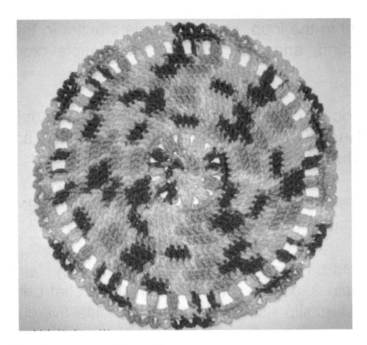

Materials: 2.5 oz. (4-ply worsted yarn)

Crochet Hook- J hook

Total Size: 13 1/2" crossways

Notes:

- Crochet tightly to adjust the size on the hook.
- Chain 2 at the start of rounds 5 to 10, it is not a stitch
- **Start cluster:** chain 2, yarn over, insert crochet hook in its space, yarn over, drag through yarn over, pull through two loops, yarn over, insert hook in the similar space, yarn over, pull through, yarn over, pull through two loops, yarn over, pull through last three loops.
- **Clusters:** yarn over, insert crochet hook in its space, pull through, yarn over, pull through two loops, yarn over, insert hook in the similar space, yarn over, pull through, yarn over, pull through two loops, yarn over, insert hook in the same place, yarn over, pull through, yarn over, pull through two loops, yarn over, pull through last four loops.

Directions:

Round 1: Ch 3 (make the 1st chain a little loose), 12 double crochet in 3rd ch from hook. Seam with a slip stitch to 1st double crochet.

Round 2: Ch 1, single crochet in the similar St as seaming, ch 2. (single crochet, ch 2) in subsequent double crochet around. Seam with a slip stitch to

1st single crochet.

Round 3: Slip stitch into the ch-2 space, beginning cluster in similar ch-2 space, ch 2. (cluster, ch 2) in subsequent ch-2 space around. Seam with a slip stitch to top of beginning cluster.

Round 4: Ch 1, two single crochet in similar st as seaming. 2 single crochet in each cluster and ch-2 space around. Seam with a slip stitch to 1st single crochet.

Round 5: Ch 2, double crochet in similar st as seaming. Double crochet in each single crochet around. Seam with a slip stitch to 1st double crochet.

Round 6: Ch 2, 2 double crochet in similar st as seaming, double crochet in subsequent 3 double crochet. *2 double crochet in subsequent double crochet, double crochet in subsequent 3 double crochet. Repeat from * around. Seam as before.

Round 7: Ch 2, 2 double crochet in similar st as seaming, double crochet in subsequent 4 double crochet. *2 double crochet in subsequent double crochet, double crochet in subsequent 4 double crochet. Repeat from * around. Seam as before.

Round 8: Ch 2, 2 double crochet in similar st as seaming, double crochet in subsequent 5 double crochet. *2 double crochet in subsequent double crochet, double crochet in subsequent 5 double crochet. Repeat from * around. Seam as before.

Round 9: Ch 2, 2 double crochet in similar st as seaming, double crochet in subsequent 6 double crochet. *2 double crochet in subsequent double crochet, double crochet in subsequent 6 double crochet. Repeat from * around. Seam as before.

Round 10: Ch 2, 2 double crochet in similar st as seaming, double crochet in subsequent 7 double crochet. *2 double crochet in subsequent double crochet, double crochet in subsequent 7 double crochet. Repeat from * around. Seam as before.

Round 11: Ch 2, 2 double crochet in similar st as seaming, double crochet in subsequent 8 double crochet. *2 double crochet in subsequent double crochet, double crochet in subsequent 8 double crochet. Repeat from * around. Seam as before.

Round 12: Beginning cluster in similar st as seaming, ch 3, skip subsequent two double crochet. *cluster in subsequent double crochet, ch 3, skip subsequent two double crochet. Repeat from * around. Seam with a slip stitch to top of beginning cluster.

Round 13: Ch 1, single crochet in similar st as seaming, three single crochet in ch-3 space. *single crochet in top of cluster, three single crochet in ch-3 space. Repeat from * around. Seam with a slip stitch to 1st single crochet.

Round 14: Ch 1, single crochet in similar st as seaming, ch 3, skip subsequent single crochet. *single crochet in subsequent single crochet, ch 3, skip subsequent single crochet. Replicate from * all the way around. Join as you do it before. Finish off.

Pattern 06: Colorful Mini Mandala

Finished Size: 4.5 inches diameter

Note: You can use different colors as per your choice.

Coaster: You can make more than one with different colors and in each coaster mandala, you will use White pulse.

Round 1: Start your choice. Using the "Magic Circle", Ch 1. Work 12 half-double-crochet in the circle. Join with sl st (slip stitch) to the top of first half-double-crochet. (12 half-double-crochet)

Round 2: Chain 1. Work 1 half-double-crochet in similar stitch as Ch 1. Work 2 half-double-crochet in each stitch around. Join to first half-double-crochet with sl st (slip stitch). (24 half-double-crochet)

Round 3: Chain 1. Work 1 half-double-crochet in similar stitch as Ch 1. *Work 1 half-double-crochet in subsequent stitch. Work 2 half-double-crochet in subsequent stitch.* Repeat from * to * around. Join to first half-double-crochet with sl st (slip stitch).

Round 4: Use White color. Chain 1. Work 1 single crochet in similar stitch as Ch 1. *Work 1 single crochet in subsequent two stitches. Work 2 single crochet in subsequent stitch. * Repeat from * to * around. Join to first single crochet with sl st (slip stitch).

Round 5: change to original color. Chain 1. Single crochet in every stitch around.

Tie up and weave all loose ends

Pattern 07: Flower Mandala

You have to make large hooks and use B color for chain 2, first round: 6 single crochet in the second chain from hook. Unite with slip stitch in first sc.

2nd round: Ch 1. You will start work in front rings, 1 single crochet in first single crochet. (1 half-double crochet. 2 double crochet. 1 half-double crochet) in subsequent single crochet. *1 single crochet in subsequent single crochet. (1 half-double crochet. 2 double crochet. 1 half-double crochet) in subsequent sc. Replicate from * once more. Do not join with slip stitch. 3 petals.

3rd round: Do not ch 1. Working in rem back rings of 1st round, 2 sc in every sc around. Join with slip stitch to first sc. 12 sc.

4th round: Ch 1. Working in front rings only, 1 sc in first sc. (1 half-double crochet. 2 double crochet. 1 half-double crochet) in subsequent sc. *1 sc in subsequent sc. (1 half-double crochet. 2 double crochet. 1 half-double crochet) in subsequent sc. Replicate from * 4 times more. Do not join with slip stitch. 6 petals.

5th round: Do not ch 1. Working in rem back rings of 3rd round, 2 sc in first sc. 1 sc in subsequent sc. (2 sc in subsequent sc. 1 sc in subsequent sc) 5 times. Join with slip stitch to first sc. 18 sc.

6th round: Ch 1. Working in front rings only, 1 sc in first sc. (1 half-double crochet. 2 double crochet. 1 half-double crochet) in subsequent sc. *1 sc in subsequent sc. (1 half-double crochet. 2 double crochet. 1 half-double crochet) in subsequent sc. Replicate from * 7 times more. Do not join with slip stitch. 9 petals.

7th round: Do not ch 1. Working in rem back rings of 5th round, 2 sc first sc. 1 sc in every of subsequent 2 sc. (2 sc in subsequent sc. 1 sc in every of subsequent 2 sc) 5 times. Join with slip stitch to first sc. 24 sc.

8th round: Ch 1. Working in front rings only, 1 sc in first sc. (1 half-double crochet. 2 double crochet. 1 half-double crochet) in subsequent sc. *1 sc in subsequent sc. (1 half-double crochet. 2 double crochet. 1 half-double crochet) in subsequent sc. Replicate from * 10 times more. Do not join with slip stitch. 12 petals.

9th round: Do not ch 1. It is time to handle rem back rings of seventh round , 2 single crochet first single crochet. 1 single crochet in every of subsequent 3 single crochet. (2 single crochet in subsequent single crochet. 1 single crochet in every of subsequent 3 single crochet) 5 times. Join with slip stitch to first single crochet. 30 single crochet.

10th round: Ch 1. Working in front rings only, 1 single crochet in first single crochet. (1 half-double crochet. 2 double crochet. 1 half-double crochet) in subsequent single crochet. *1 single crochet in subsequent single crochet. (1 half-double crochet. 2 double crochet. 1 half-double crochet) in subsequent single crochet. Replicate from * 13 times more. Join with slip stitch to first single crochet. Fasten off. It will be 15 petals.

Pattern 08: Black Mandala

- Worsted Weight yarn: 8ply black
- Crochet hook: 4mm
- Needles to weave ends

Directions:

Round 1 (Colour A): Make one slip-knot, chain four, and join with a slip-stitch to initiate the. Ch2, and work 11 double crochet (double crochet) into the middle of the ring. Join to the top of the initial ch2 with a slip-stitch, and fasten off Colour A.

Round 2 (Colour B): Use B color, chain 2, and work 1half-double-crochet (half-double crochet) into a similar place. Work 2half-double-crochet into each stitch of the previous round. Join to top of initial ch2 with a slip-stitch, and fasten off Colour B.

Round 3 (Black): Flip the side of the coaster, and join Black. Chain2, one half-double-crochet into a similar place. *1half-double-crochet in next stitch, then 2half-double-crochet in next stitch,* replicate from * to * until one stitch remains, 1half-double-crochet in final stitch. Join to top of initial ch2 with a slip-stitch.

Round 4: Ch2, 1half-double-crochet into a similar place. *1half-double-crochet, 1half-double-crochet, 2half-double-crochet,* replicate until one stitch remains, half-double-crochet in final stitch. Note: the 2half-double-crochet will fall between the 2half-double-crochet of the previous round. Seam to the top of initial ch2 with a slip-stitch.

Round 5: Ch2, 1half-double-crochet into a similar place. *1half-double-crochet, 1half-double-crochet, 1half-double-crochet, 2half-double-crochet,* replicate until

1 stitch remains, 1half-double-crochet. Join to top of initial ch2 with a slip-stitch.

Round 6: Ch1, 1single crochet into a similar place. Single crochet into each stitch of the previous round. Join to first single crochet with a slip-stitch.

Tie up yarn, weave all its ends.

Pattern 09: Mandala Blanket

- **Yarn: 104 yds or .95 m**
- **A Color: 4 balls**
- **B color: 2 balls**
- **C color: 2 balls**
- **D color: 2 Balls**
- **E Color: 2 balls**
- **F Color: 2 balls**
- **9mm or N/15 crochet hook**

Measurements: 185 cm or 73 inches in diameter

Directions:

Stripe Perfectly

Start with A color - 2 rounds. Use B color - 1 round. Use C color - 1 rnd. Use d color - 1 rnd. Use E color - 1 rnd. Use F color - 1 rnd.

These seven rounds to form Stripe perfectly.

Notes: You will use a new color for joining and work to last two loops on the hook. Yarn over the hook with a fresh color and drag through two loops on the crochet hook.

- Ch 3 at beg of round counts as a double crochet. Ch 4 at beg of round counts as treble.

- Link all rounds with sl st to first single crochet or top of ch 3 (4).

Start with A color, ch 2.

Proceed in Strebleipe Pat as follows:

1st round: 10 single crochet in 2nd ch from hook. Link with sl st to the top of ch 3. 10 single crochet.

2nd round: Ch 3. 1 double crochet in similar space as sl st. 2 double crochet in every double crochet around. Link B. 20 double crochet.

3rd round: Use B color, ch 1. *1 single crochet in subsequent double crochet. Two single crochet in subsequent double crochet. Replicate from * around. Link C. 30 single crochet.

4th round: Use C color, ch 4. 1 treble in every of subsequent two single crochet. *2 treble in subsequent single crochet. One treble in every of subsequent two single crochet. Replicate from * around. Link D. 40 treble.

5th round: Use d color, ch 1. *2 single crochet in the subsequent treble. One single crochet in every of subsequent three trebles. Replicate from * around. Link E. 50 single crochet.

6th round: Use E color, ch 3. one double crochet in subsequent single crochet. *2 double crochet in subsequent single crochet. One double crochet in every of subsequent four single crochet. Replicate from * to last two single crochet. One double crochet in every of last two single crochet. Link F. 60 double crochet.

7th round: Use F color, ch 1. *2 single crochet in subsequent double crochet. One single crochet in every of subsequent five double crochet. Replicate from * around. Link A. 70 single crochet.

8th round: Start with A color, ch 4. 1 treble in every of subsequent two single crochet. *2 treble in subsequent single crochet. One treble in every of subsequent six single crochet. Replicate from * to last four single crochet. Two treble in subsequent single crochet. One treble in every of last three single crochet. Link. 80 treble.

9th round: Ch 1. *2 single crochet in the subsequent treble. One single crochet in every of subsequent seven trebles. Replicate from * around. Link B. 90 single crochet.

10th round: Use B color, ch 3. one double crochet in every of subsequent two single crochet. *2 double crochet in subsequent single crochet. One double crochet in every of following eight single crochet. Replicate from * to last six single crochet. Two double crochet in subsequent single crochet. One double crochet in every of last five single crochet. Link C. 100 double crochet.

11th round: Use C color, ch 1. *2 single crochet in subsequent double crochet. One single crochet in every of subsequent nine double crochet. Replicate from * around. Link D. 110 single crochet.

12th round: Use d color, ch 4. 1 treble in every of subsequent three single crochet. *2 treble in subsequent single crochet. One treble in every of subsequent ten single crochet. Replicate from * to last seven single crochet. Two treble in subsequent single crochet. One treble in every of last six single crochet. Link E. 120 treble.

13th round: Use e color, ch 1. *2 single crochet in the subsequent treble. One single crochet in every of subsequent 11 trebles. Replicate from * around. Link F. 130 single crochet.

14th round: Use F color, ch 3. one double crochet in every of subsequent four single crochet. *2 double crochet in following single crochet. One double crochet in every of subsequent 12 single crochet. Replicate from * to last eight single crochet. Two double crochet in subsequent single crochet. One double crochet in every of last seven single crochet. Link A. 140 double crochet.

15th round: Start with A color, ch 1. *2 single crochet in subsequent double crochet. One single crochet in every of subsequent 13 double crochet. Replicate from * around. Link. 150 single crochet.

16th round: Ch 4. 1 treble in every of subsequent five single crochet. *2 treble in subsequent single crochet. One treble in every of subsequent 14 single crochet. Replicate from * to last nine single crochet. Two treble in subsequent single crochet. One treble in every of last eight single crochet. Link B. 160 treble.

Continue in a similar manner and include ten stitches in every round and work in the following sequence: single crochet round, double crochet round, single crochet round, treble round, until work measures almost 70" (178 cm) diameter. Tie-up.

Pattern 10: Mandala Pouch

- **Weight of Yarn:** Lace (33 to 40 stitches to four inches) (0)
- **Crochet Thread:** 8 Size Yarn
- **Hook:** Crochet hook of steel 2.20mm or 3 size hook
- **Lace ribbon:** 18 inches long to tie
- **Circumference:** 2 ¾ inches and Height: 3 ¾ inches

Special Stitches Instructions:

2dc-bobble: Yo (yarn over), insert crochet hook in stitch and pull yarn thread from side to side, yo and draw through two loops on crochet hook, Yo, put in in similar stitch and pull this thread through, yarn over and draw through two loops on hook, yarn over and draw through all three loops on crochet hook.)

dc2tog: Yarn over, put in crochet hook in stitch and draw thread through, yarn over and pull through two loops on hook, Yarn over, insert in subsequent stitch and drag thread through, yarn over and draw through two loops on crochet hook, yarn over and draw through all three loops on crochet hook.)

Directions:

Use cotton thread of size 8

chain 3 (consider as 1 double crochet).

Round 1: 11 double crochet in the initial chain (12 double crochet made). Slip stitch in top of initial double crochet to join.

Round 2: Chain 3, double crochet in same st, 2 double crochet in every double crochet, slip stitch in top of initial double crochet to join. (24 double crochet)

Round 3: Chain 3, *chain 1, double crochet in subsequent double crochet, replicate from * all around ending with chain 1, slip stitch in top of initial double crochet to join.

Round 4: Chain 3, double crochet in same double crochet, *chain 2, 2double crochet-bobble in subsequent double crochet, replicate from * all around ending with chain 2, slip stitch in top of initial double crochet to join.

Round 5: *Chain 7, skip 1 bobble, single crochet in a subsequent bobble, replicate from * all around. (12 chain-7 loops made)

Round 6: Slip stitch to the corner of chain-7 loop, chain 3 (consider as 1 double crochet), 6 double crochet in the loop, *chain 2, 7 double crochet in the subsequent loop, replicate from * all around, ending with chain 2, slip stitch in initial double crochet to join.

Round 7: Chain 3, double crochet in subsequent 6 double crochet, *chain 2, double crochet in subsequent 7 double crochet, skip 2-chain space, double crochet in subsequent 7 double crochet, replicate from * all around ending with slip stitch in initial double crochet to join.

Round 8: Slip stitch to top of 2nd double crochet, chain 3, double crochet in subsequent 5 double crochet, *chain 3, double crochet in subsequent 6 double crochet, skip 2 double crochet, double crochet in subsequent 6 double crochet, replicate from * all around ending with slip stitch in initial double crochet to join.

Round 9: Slip stitch to top of 2nd double crochet, chain 3, double crochet in subsequent 4 double crochet, *chain 3, 5 double crochet in chain-3 space, chain 3, double crochet in subsequent 5 double crochet, skip 2 double crochet, double crochet in subsequent 5 double crochet, replicate from * all around, ending with slip stitch in initial double crochet to join.

Round 10: Slip stitch to top of 2nd double crochet, chain 3, double crochet in subsequent 3 double crochet, *chain 3, [double crochet in subsequent double crochet, chain 1] 4 times, double crochet in subsequent double crochet, chain 3, double crochet in subsequent 4 double crochet, skip 2 double crochet, double crochet in subsequent 4 double crochet, replicate from * all around, ending with slip stitch in initial double crochet to join.

Round 11: Slip stitch to top of 2nd double crochet, chain 3, double crochet in subsequent 2 double crochet, *chain 3, skip chain-3 space[single crochet in chain-1 loop, chain 3] 3 times, single crochet in last chain-1 loop, chain 3, double crochet in subsequent 3 double crochet, skip 2 double crochet, double crochet in subsequent 3 double crochet, replicate from * all around, ending with slip stitch in initial double crochet to join.

Round 12: Slip stitch to top of 2nd double crochet, chain 3, double crochet in subsequent double crochet, *chain 3, skip chain-3 space, [single crochet in chain-3 loop, chain 3] 2 times, single crochet in last chain-3 loop, chain 3, double crochet in subsequent 2 double crochet, skip 2 double crochet, double crochet in subsequent 2 double crochet, replicate from * all around, ending with slip stitch in initial double crochet to join.

Round 13: Chain 3, double crochet in subsequent double crochet, *chain 3, skip chain-3 space, single crochet in chain-3 loop, chain 3, single crochet in subsequent chain-3 loop, chain 3, double crochet2tog in subsequent 2 double crochet, chain 5, double crochet2tog in subsequent 2 double crochet, replicate from * all around, ending with chain 5, slip stitch in top of initial double crochet to join.

Round 14: Chain 6 (make 1 double crochet, chain 3), *skip chain-3 space, single crochet in chain-3 loop, chain 3, 7 double crochet in the chain-5 loop, chain 3, replicate from * all around ending with 6 double crochet in last chain-5 loop. Slip stitch in top of double crochet (3rd chain of chain 6) to join.

Round 15: Chain 6 (make 1 double crochet, chain 3), *skip (3 chain, single crochet, 3 chain), double crochet in subsequent double crochet, [chain 1, double crochet in subsequent double crochet] 6 times, chain 3, replicate from * all around ending with chain 1, slip stitch in top of initial double crochet to join.

Round 16: Slip stitch to chain-1 space, *chain 3, double crochet in chain-3 space, [chain 3, single crochet in chain-1 space] 6 times, replicate from * all around.

Round 17: Slip stitch up chain 3 to tip of double crochet, chain 3, 2 double crochet in same double crochet, *[chain 3, single crochet in chain-3 loop] 5 times, chain 3, 3 double crochet in subsequent double crochet, replicate from * all around ending with chain 3, slip stitch in initial double crochet to join.

Round 18: Chain 4 (consider as 1 double crochet, chain 1), double crochet in subsequent double crochet, chain 1, double crochet in subsequent double crochet, *[chain 3, single crochet in chain-3 loop] 4 times, chain 3, [double crochet in subsequent double crochet, chain 1] 2 times, double crochet in subsequent double crochet, replicate from * all around ending with chain 3, slip stitch in initial double crochet in to join.

Round 19: Chain 3, double crochet in same double crochet, *[chain 1, 2 double crochet in subsequent double crochet] 2 times, [chain 3, single crochet in chain-3 loop] 3 times, chain 3, 2 double crochet in subsequent double crochet, replicate from * all around, ending with chain 3, slip stitch in initial double crochet to join.

Round 20: Chain 3, double crochet in same double crochet, *[chain 1, 2 double crochet in subsequent double crochet] 5 times, [chain 3, single crochet in chain-3 loop] 2 times, chain 3, 2 double crochet in subsequent double crochet, replicate from * all around, ending with chain 3, slip stitch in initial double crochet to join. (You should have 12 2-double crochet groups in every single each scallop)

Round 21: Chain 3, double crochet in subsequent double crochet, *[chain 3, slip stitch in 3rd chain from hook to make picot, double crochet2tog in subsequent 2 double crochet] 5 times, chain 3, single crochet in chain-3 loop, picot, chain 3, double crochet2tog in subsequent 2 double crochet, replicate from * all around, ending with chain 3, slip stitch in initial double crochet to join. Tie up.

Dry and block. Use lace ribbon to weave 14 rounds and keep ribbon behind 7 (dc) double crochet group. Tie all ends of lace ribbon and make a knot as per your desire.

Pattern 11: Mandala Bag for Market

- 2 balls of yarn
- Crochet hook: I hook or 5.5mm
- Yarn needle and scissors

Directions:

- Chain 2

- Rnd 1: Work 6 single crochet in the first chain

- Rnd 2: Work 2 single crochet in every single crochet around - 12 st

- Rnd 3: *2 single crochet in subsequent st, single crochet in subsequent st, replicate from * around - 18 st

- Rnd 4: *2 single crochet in subsequent st, single crochet in every of subsequent two stitches, replicate from * around - 24 stitches

- Rnd 5: *2 single crochet in subsequent st, single crochet in every of subsequent three stitches, replicate from * around - 30 stitches

- Rnd 6: *2 single crochet in subsequent st, single crochet in every of subsequent four stitches, replicate from * around - 36 stitches

- Rnd 7: *2 single crochet in subsequent st, single crochet in every of subsequent five stitches, replicate from * around - 42 stitches

- Rnd 8: *2 single crochet in subsequent st, single crochet in every of subsequent six stitches, replicate from * around - 48 stitches

- Rnd 9: *2 single crochet in subsequent st, single crochet in every of subsequent seven stitches, replicate from * around - 54 stitches

- Rnd 10: half-double-crochet -54 st

It is time to form a lattice, chain 5, skip two stitches, single crochet, replicate from * the last single crochet should be in the initial single crochet

*chain 6, single crochet to the middle of the subsequent loop, replicate from * till conclusion of row

*chain 7, single crochet to the middle of the subsequent loop, replicate from * until conclusion of your row

*chain 8, single crochet to the middle of the subsequent loop, replicate from * until the end of your row

*chain 9, single crochet to the midst of the subsequent loop, replicate from *work seven rows of chain 9

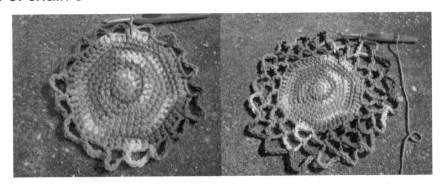

*Ch 5, single crochet to middle of the subsequent loop, replicate from *until the end

single crochet into chain 5 row and single crochet 2 to 3 extra rows

Finish the top row and mark the place of handles with single crochet. To make a handle, you can crochet 3 to 4 rows of single crochet, or you can get your desired length. Weave all ends, and the bag is ready.

Pattern 12: Mandala Shoulder Bag

- Crochet Hook: Size H
- Fabric for Cotton Lining: 1 yd
- Worsted Yarn: 1 ball or more
- Matching thread and needle

Notes:

Chain three at the finishing of every row will be counted as the first double crochet of the subsequent row.

Pattern:

Chain 4; join with a slip stitch to form a ring.

Round 1: Chain 3 to count as the first dc, work 7 more dc in the ring; chain 3, flip. (8 dc)

Round 2: Dc in the first dc, 2 dc in every remaining dc across; chain 3, flip. (16 dc)

Round 3: Replicate round 2. (32 dc)

Round 4: Dc in the first dc and in every dc across, 2 dc in the top of the flipping chain; chain 3, flip. (34 dc) (Increase at every finishing off the round.)

Round 5: Replicate round 4. (36 dc)

Round 6: Replicate round 2. (72 dc)

Round 7: Replicate round 4. (74 dc)

Round 8: Replicate round 4. (76 dc)

Round 9: Replicate round 4. (78 dc)

Round 10: Replicate round 4. (80 dc)

Round 11: Dc in the first dc (dc in the subsequent dc, 2 dc in the subsequent dc) across, dc in the flipping chain; chain 3, flip. (120 dc)

Round 12: Replicate round 4. (122 dc)

Round 13: Replicate round 4. (124 dc)

Round 14: Replicate round 4. (126 dc)

Round 15: Replicate round 4. (128 dc)

Round 16: Replicate round 4. (130 dc) Tie up. Weave in all ends.

Handle

Chain 220; being careful not to twist chain, join with a slip stitch to the first chain.

Round 1: Chain 3 to count as the first double crochet, double crochet in every chain around; join with a slip stitch to the top of the beginning chain 3. (220 double crochet)

Round 2: Replicate round 1.

Note: You will need additional yarn if you want to make 5 rows.

Rounds 3 to 5: Replicate round 1.

Assembly

Iron every crocheted part to block. If you want to line your bag, you can lay the crocheted parts of the fabric to trace the pattern of crocheted parts. Make sure to add seam allowance and cut along with traced line. Sew this lining to fit in the bag and flip its inside out. Slip stitch row 16 of one crocheted piece pieces to 130 stitches of row 5 of a handle, then carry on working slip stitch's in the leftover 90 handle stitches; seam with a slip stitch to the initial slip stitch; Tie up. Slip stitch row 16 of the other bag piece to 130 stitches of all free loops of the base chain of this handle, carry on working a slip stitch in the left over 90 handle stitches; seam with a slip stitch to the initial slip stitch; Tie up. Weave its ends.

Insert lining into your bag and whip stitch to the handle and opening of the bag. You can sew inside of the bag, after the initial ring.

Conclusion

Try these mandala patterns that are beautiful and easy to crochet. Step-by-step guidance is available with each pattern. You can use these patterns to design bags and gifts for your friends and family members.

Crochet Pillow:
10 Brilliant Crochet Pillow Cases To Make Your Home Super Cozy

Introduction

Classic and stylish pillow covers with striking designs changes the look of place all together. They bring an ideal make over to interior and spruces up the décor of your room. These decorative crafts are adorable and have impact of lively and vibrant surroundings.

Crocheting has been practiced many years. They are being used to make hats, Beanies, jerseys, scarves and different other accessories plus frocks, dresses, blankets etc. It is basically a method of fabric creation. Crochet hook is used to inter lock the strands of thread, yarn or any other material. Different sort of stitches and patterns are used to create different crochet designs.

This book will get you through ten different crochet patterns or stitches for making cushion pillows. Everything you need to know about them is covered.

All you need to crochet is a crochet hook, some yarn and a pair of scissors, this eBook and that's set. Crochet hand books are also available to help you in making different patterns. Further crochet tutorials are available on internet, which will help you in learning different techniques and methods to be expert in it. These tutorials along with this book will be your ultimate solution to crochet pillows.

Remember don't lose heart on holding hook and if you are not able to dangle it. Practice again and again and that will not only make you capable of doing it but also to be an expert in it. Consider the following chart that will help you throughout the book to understand abbreviations. These abbreviations will be repeated throughout the book.

FREQUENTLY USED ABBREVIATIONS

beg	beginning
CC	contrast color
ch(s)	chain(s)
ch sp	chain space
cl(s)	cluster(s)
cont	continue
dc	double crochet
dec(ing)	decrease(ing)
ea	each
est	established
hdc	half double crochet
hk	hook
in(s)	inch(es)
inc(ing)	increase(ing)
MC	main color
pat st	pattern stitch
prev	previous
rem(ing)	remain(ing)
rep(s)	repeat(s)
rnd	round
RS	right side
sc	single crochet
sk	skip
sl	slip
sl st	slip stitch
sp(s)	space(s)
st(s)	stitch(es)
tog	together
tr	treble crochet
WS	wrong side
YO	yarn over

Here we will be discussing about ten different techniques and design to give you efficiency over versatile crochet designs.

Design no. 1 Checkerboard Pillow crochet Pattern

Requirements

- 9 oz weight yarn (one color)
- 8 oz weight yarn(second color)
- crochet hook
- needle
- 14" Pillow polyester for stuffing

(Here cornmeal and burgundy colors have been used as 1st and 2nd color respectively, but you may alter according to your choice.

instructions:

Strip A: (make 6)

Row 1: Take 1st selected color, start with ch and then single crochet in subsequent ch as of the hook and in every ch crossways, ch 1, twist

Rows 2-8: Single crochet in every sc crossways, ch 1, twist

Row 9: Single crochet in every sc crossways, shift to second color, ch 1, twist

Rows 10-17: Single crochet in every sc crossways, ch 1, twist

Row 18: Single crochet in every Sc crossways, change to first color, ch 1, twist

Row 19-26: Single crochet in every sc crossways, ch 1, twist

Row 27: Single crochet in every sc crossways, again shift to second color, ch 1, twist

Rows 28-35: Single crochet in every sc crossways, ch 1, twist

Row 36: Single crochet in every sc crossways, change to first color, ch 1, twist

Rows 37-44: Single crochet in every sc crossways, ch 1, twist

Row 45: Single crochet in every sc crossways, terminate off, and finally interlace in loose ends.

Strip B: (4)
Row 1: Take second color, ch 10, then single crochet in other ch as of hook and into every ch crossways, ch 1, and then twist

Rows 2-8: Single crochet in every sc crossways, ch 1, twist

Row 9: Single crochet in every sc crossways, change to first color, ch 1, twist

Rows 10-17: Single crochet in every sc crossways, ch 1, twist

Row 18: Single crochet in every Sc crossways, change to second color, ch 1, twist

Row 19-26: Single crochet in every sc crossways, ch 1, twist

Row 27: Single crochet in every sc crossways, change to first color, ch 1, twist

Rows 28-35: Single crochet in every sc crossways, ch 1, twist

Row 36: Single crochet in every sc crossways, change to second color, ch 1, twist

Rows 37-44: Single crochet in every sc crossways, ch 1, twist

Row 45: Single crochet in every sc crossways, finish off, again weave in wobbly ends.

Pillow Assembling and making Border:
Round 1: Put the two accomplished panels incorrect sides jointly. With second color yarn and operating through these two thicknesses and then sc two panels in concert all the length of three sides. Keep the checker squares creased up. Insert pillow form, sc fourth side closed, ch 1, and twist.

Round 2: Single crochet in every single crochet in the region of working 3 single crochet in corners, ch 1, twist

Rnd 3: RSingle crochet in every single crochet in the region of working 3 RSingle crochet in corners, stop it and interlace in slack ends.

Your adorable checker cushion is ready.

Design no. 2 Circular pillow at top

Requirements

- Yarn: four balls of first color and three balls of second color.
- Crochet Hook 2 / 0.
- A filling or polyester, Diameter: 15 inches
- GAUGE: 5 single crochet to make one inch; two double crochet and 1 single crochet Row to make 11 ¼ inches.

Method

Start with the first color at the middle, chain 5

1st round: 25 treble in 5th ch from hook, insert hook in top of starting chain, drop first color, attach second color and drag loop over chain and loop on crochet hook, now start joining round and keep on changing color in this way.

2nd round: 2 single crochet in similar place as slip stitch (1 st increased), * single crochet in subsequent treble, 2 single crochet in subsequent treble. Replicate from * around. Second color yarn, pick up first color.

3rd round: Ch 3, double crochet in similar place as slip stitch, double crochet in every single crochet, rising 12 double crochet equally in the similar order, drop second color, pick up first color and then Join.

4th round: Here Single crochet in similar position as slip stitch, single crochet in subsequent 2 double crochet, * thread over, insert hook into single crochet on previous single crochet round, draw loop throughout, twice; thread over and draw through all loops on hook, skip double crochet straight at the rear of puff st, single crochet in subsequent 3 double crochet. Replicate from * around, drop second color and pick up first color and finally join.

5th round: To be following in a way like 3rd round.

6th round: Single crochet in every single crochet around, escalating 19 single crochet uniformly around.

7th and 8th rounds: duplicate last 2 rounds.

9th round: Replicate 3rd round in similar way.
10th round: Then replicate 4th round similarly.

11th to 16th rounds including: Replicate 5th round to 10th round incl.

17th to 21st rounds including: Replicate 5th to 9th rounds incl.

At end of **last round,** join them and then break off the yarn.

Similarly make another piece. Keep both sides facing wrong and then work through both of the thicknesses to join them, attach second color to any double crochet, single crochet in equivalent position, single crochet in every double crochet about to within 10 inches from first single crochet, put in pillow and single crochet in every lasting double crochet. Join and again break off. And eye catching crochet cushion is ready.

Design no. 3 Second round pillow

Requirements:

- Yarn: 3 balls of one color and 2 balls of second.
- Crochet Hook
- 15" pillow foam
- GAUGE: 1" by 3 puff sts and approximately 4 rnds make 1½ inches.

Method:

In this method, initiate it with starting from the center with second color, ch 2.

1st rnd: 7 single crochet in 2nd ch as of hook and then connect.

2nd rnd: 2 single crochet in every sc around and again unite.

3rd rnd: Ch 3. Do it three times and thread above and sketch through all loops lying on hook. Build a puff st in every sc all around and then link to peak of first puff st.

4th rnd: Single crochet in rear loop of every puff st and in every ch around. Unite and break off.

5th rnd: Attach first color to similar place as slip stitch, ch 3, make a puff st in every sc and then unite.

6th rnd: Sc similar as slip stitch, * single crochet in next ch (1 single crochet increased), single crochet in next 2 puff sts. Repeat from * around. Combine and split off.

7th rnd: Unite second color to first sc and do again 5th rnd.

8th rnd: Single crochet in every sc around, mounting 14 sc consistently around. Unite and break off.

Do again last 2 rnds, change color on every added rnd until 18 rnds.

19th rnd: Single crochet in every sc around and increases it up to the demand and then unite.

Repeat l9th rnd until piece measures equal size as that of pillow.

After last rnd, unite and split off.

Other piece has to be made in the similar way. After completing, with incorrect sides opposite and working along both, attach Claret to any sc, sc directly in the region of within l0 inches of first sc, pop in pillow and single crochet intimately around left over periphery. Fasten together and split off. And add the cushion to enhance your home's interior looks.

Design no. 4 Square Yellow Pillow

Requirements

- Yarn: 6 balls any color. I selected Yellow
- Crochet Hook
- 14 inches pillow foam of square shape.
- GAUGE: 1 shell and 2 sc make 1 ¾ inches

From the bottom, start making a chain 12 inches in length.

Method:

1st Row: Single crochet in 2nd ch as of hook, * skip 2 ch, 5 dc in subsequent ch, hop 2 ch, single crochet in after that ch,. Replicate from * crossways until there are 7 shells on Row, ending with an sc, hop 2 ch, 3 double crochet in preceding ch . Cut the left over chain. Ch 1, flip.

2nd Row: Single crochet in first dc, * shell in next sc, single crochet in center dc of subsequent shell. Do again from * transversely, till revery half shell in end sc. Ch 1. Flip. Do again 2nd Row until piece is finalized into a square.

For edging:

1st rnd: Sc closely around, making 3 single crochet in every corner.

2nd rnd: Single crochet in every sc around, making 3 single crochet in middle sc of every corner.

Do again 2nd rnd until the piece procedures 14 inch square. Unite it and then break off.

Other piece is to be made in the similar way. With incorrect sides in front of and functioning through both thicknesses, fasten the thread to some corner, single crochet in every sc around three sides, pop in pillow and sc crossways the left over side. Unite and smash off.

Decorate them in lounge and captivate your visitor's focus.

Design no. 5

This is another beautiful design for a crochet. All stitches in it are double crochet, chain or a skipped space, and it is named as filet crochet.

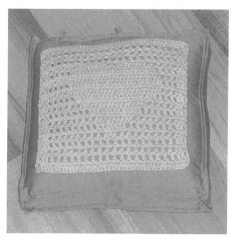

Level: Intermediate

Requirements:

- 2 oz cotton worsted yarn
- crochet hook of size E/4 (3.50 mm)

Instructions:

Chain 45

Row 1: sk first 3 ch , dc in second chain and across (42 sts)

Follow the chart for the rest of the directions.

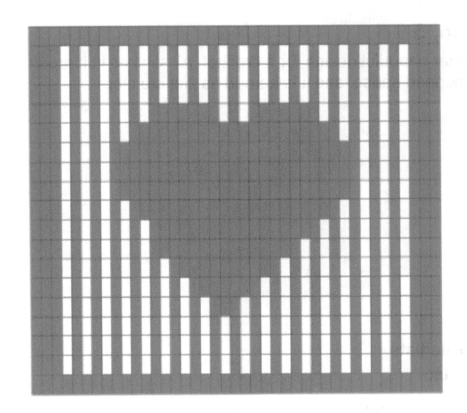

Design no. 6 Diagonal pillow

Pillow size: 14" x 14"

Requirements:

- Yarn: 3 balls of one color and 3 balls of second chosen color.
- Crochet Hook 3.5mm in size
- Yarn needle
- Pillow form of 14 inches.
- GAUGE: 2" in pattern which would be equal to 4 shells..

Method:

Pillow Front

Row 1 (work from Right Side): With A, ch 6, dc in 4th ch from hook, dc in next 2 ch; flip – 1 shell.

Row 2: Ch 6, dc in 4th ch initiating from hook, dc in next 2 ch – starting shell made; (slip st, ch 3, 3 dc) all over ch-3 of previous row shells made; flip – 2 shells.

Row 3: Starting shell, * shell; repeat from * across changing to B in last dc; flip – 3 shells.

Row 4: Starting shell, * shell; repeat from * across; flip.

Repeat Row 4 for pattern, increasing 1 shell every row, in the appropriate color chain:– 22 shells at finish of preceding row.

Row 23: With A, ch 1, slip st in first 3 dc, * shell; repeat from * to last shell; slide st in last ch-3 changing to B; flip – 21 shells.

Row 24: Ch 1, slip st in first 3 dc, * shell; do it again from * to end shell; slip st in last ch-3 space; go round – 20 shells.

Duplicate Row 24 for pattern, lessening 1 shell every row, in the appropriate color sequence. Fasten off. Back Work similar as Front EXCEPT reverse the colors using first color in place of second color and second color in place of first color.

Assemblage

Keeping wrong sides together and working through thicknesses, unite A and effort 1 round sc consistently in the region of 3 sides.

Slot in pillow foam; complete sc round.

Unite with a slip st in first sc. Fasten off. And finally it would be like this.

Get reminded of abbreviations again.

Design no. 7

Required materials

It will be a 14" **Pillow.**

- 3 balls of yarn of selected color
- **Hook of** U.S. Size H-8 [5mm].
- 14" or 16" sized pillow forms.
- **GAUGES: In sc rnds** - 14 sts = 4"; 18 rnds = 4". **Motif** – 3¾" square.

Check the gauge first. Utilize any size hook to get the gauges given.

FRONT-Motif (Make 9)-Rnd 1:
Ch 2; 8 single crochet in 2nd ch by hook and unite with a slip stitch to first sc.

Rnd 2: Ch 2; *holding at back last lp on hook, 2 dc in similar sc as joining, yo and through all 3 lps on hook* – **beg cl (cluster)** completed, *[ch 3; holding back last lp on hook, 3 double crochet in subsequent sc, yo and from side to side all 4 lps on hook* – **cl** made] 7 times; ch 1, dc in top of beg cl to connect and form last lp – 8 cl.

Rnd 3: Ch 1, 3 sc above dc, [5 single crochet in subsequent ch-3 sp] 7 times, 2 sc above ch-1; connect with a slip stitch to first sc.

Rnd 4: Ch 1, single crochet in similar sc as unification, * ch 4, skip subsequent 4 sc, single crochet in after that sc, ch 8, skip then 4 sc **, single crochet in subsequent sc; rep from * around, end at **; unite to first sc.

Rnd 5: Ch 1, * 4 single crochet in ch-4 lp, (5 sc, ch 2, 5 sc) all in ch-8 lp; rep from * around; connect and then tie up off. Interlace in ends.

Edging: Fasten together thread in last sc **ahead of** any corner.

Rnd 1: Ch 3, * 3 double crochet in corner sp, dc in every sc to subsequent corner, rep from * in the region of; join to top of ch-3 – 180 sts.

Rnd 2: Ch 3, dc in every dc around; unite and the Fasten off.

Back:
Create one motif similar as for front but do not tie up off at Rnd 5 ending .

Rnd 6: Ch 3, dc in subsequent sc and in all sc to corner sp, * all in corner sp, dc in every sc crossways; rep from * all around in that region, link to top of ch-3 – 18 sts between corner sps.

Rnd 7: Ch 3, dc in subsequent dc and all dc to corner, * (dc, ch 2, dc) everyone in corner sp, dc in every dc across; rep from * around; join – 20 sts between corner sps.

Rnd 8: Ch 3, dc in subsequent dc and every dc to corner, * (2 dc, ch 2, 2 dc) all in corner sp, dc in every dc crossways; rep from * all around and then join – 24 sts between corner sps.

Rnd 9: Rep Rnd 7 – 26 sts between corner sps.

Rnds 10, 11, 12, and 13: Follow similar as in Rnd 8 – 42 sts among corner sps at end of Rnd 13.

Rnd 14: Ch 3, dc in subsequent dc and every dc to corner, * 3 double crochet in corner sp, dc in every dc crossways; rep from * around; join – 180 sts around. Fasten off. Weave all ends.

WINDING UP:
Take wrong sides' jointly and match st for st, sc through both layers around front and back, popping in pillow form before closing last side and fasten together. Tie up.
And let your visitors remember you with the mesmerizing look of your living area.

Design no. 8 Simple Round pillow

Materials

- Yarn hook
- 7 oz of worsted weight of selected color of yarn

Procedure

If you have to make Round pillow form, you require making two pieces of them for front and back

Ch 4, slip stitch tog to form a ring.

Round 1: Ch 3, 13 double crochet in circle, slip stitch tog.

Rnd 2: Ch 3, dc in similar st, 2 dc in every st around, slip stitch tog.

Round 3: Ch 3, dc in similar st, *dc in subsequent 2 sts, 2dc. Replicate from * all around. Slip stitch tog.

Round 4: Ch 3, dc in similar st, *dc in subsequent 2 sts, 2dc. Replicate from * all around. Slip stitch tog.

Round 5: Ch 3, dc in similar st, *dc in subsequent 3 sts, 2dc. Repeat from * all around. Slip stitch tog.

Round 6: Ch 3, dc in similar st, *dc in subsequent 4 sts, 2dc. Repeat from * all around. Slip stitch tog.

Round 7: Ch 3, dc in similar st, *dc in subsequent 5 sts, 2dc. Repeat from * all around. Slip stitch tog.

Round 8: Ch 3, dc in similar st, *dc in subsequent 6 sts, 2dc. Repeat from * all around. Slip stitch tog.

Round 9: Ch 3, dc in similar st, *dc in subsequent 6 sts, 2dc. Repeat from * all around. Slip stitch tog.

Round 10: Ch 3, dc in similar st, *dc in subsequent 10 sts, 2dc. Repeat from * all around. Slip stitch tog.

Round 11: Ch 3, dc in similar st, dc in every st all around. Slip stitch tog.

Round 12: Replicate Round 11. tie off and then weave in end. On 2nd round, do not tie off.

Slip stitch tog opposite sides of pillow rounds. After halfway done, slip pillow foam between them. Then finish slip stitch all around. Fasten off and weave in end.

Design no. 9 Ribbon laced crochet cushion

Materials

- Yarn 1 skein of requires color
- Crochet Hook: H/8 [5.00mm]
- 12"-square pillow form
- fabric to match yarn of about size two 13" squares;
- thread for sewing
- needle
- Any colored ribbon ⅝"- I selected wide purple velvet ribbon, 27" length
- Again any colored ribbon I selected ⅝"-wide green velvet ribbon of lengths 14" and 46"
- 3"square piece of cardboard.
- GAUGE: Rounds 1–3 of pattern to make size 4¼" x 4¼".

Front = 12" square prior to amalgamation. Make sure to check the Gauge. Use any size needles to get the gauge.

Directions:

PATTERN STITCH Shell: Work 5 dc in specified st. FRONT Ch 4. Unite with slip stitch in first ch to form a ring.

Rnd 1 (right side): Ch 3 (counts as dc), work 15 dc in ring – 16 dc. Unite with slip stitch in 3rd chain of beginning ch-3.

Rnd 2: Ch 1, single crochet in similar ch as uniting, single crochet in subsequent 2 dc; *(sc, ch 2, sc) in subsequent dc, single crochet in subsequent 3 dc; replicate from * 2 times further (sc, ch 2, sc) in very last dc – 20 sc and 4 corner chain 2 spaces. Unite with slip stitch in beginning sc.

Rnd 3: Ch 4 (taken as double crochet and chain-1 sp), sk subsequent sc, dc in subsequent sc; *ch 1, sk subsequent sc, (dc, ch 1, dc, ch 2, dc, ch 1, dc) in corner ch-2 sp**; [ch 1, sk subsequent sc, dc in subsequent sc] twice*; replicate from * to * around, ending final replicate at **; ch 1, sk last sc – 24 dc, 20 ch-1 sps and 4 corner chain 2 spaces. Unite with slip stitch in 3rd chain of in start of ch-4.

Rnd 4: Chain 4 (taken as treble); *(2 treble, chain 2, 2 treble) in subsequent chain-1 sp, tr in subsequent dc, dc in subsequent chain-1 space and in subsequent dc, hdc in subsequent ch-1 sp, single crochet in subsequent dc, slip stitch in subsequent chain-2 sp, single crochet in subsequent dc, hdc in subsequent chain-1 sp, dc in subsequent dc and in subsequent chain-1sp**; tr in subsequent dc; replicate from * around, ending final replicate at ** - 24 tr, 16 dc, 8 hdc, 8 sc, 4 slip stitchs and 4 corner chain 2 spaces. Unite with slip stitch in 4th ch of beginning ch-4.

Rnd 5: Ch 1, single crochet in similar ch as uniteing and in every stitch around, working (sc, ch 2, sc) in every corner ch-2 sp – 68 sc and 4 corner chain 2 spaces. Unite with slip stitch in first sc. Ch 4 (it will be taken as double crochet and chain-1 sp on subsequent round), flip.

Rnd 6: (wrong side) Sk first sc, dc in subsequent sc; *ch 1, sk subsequent sc**, dc in subsequent sc; replicate from * all around, functioning (dc, ch 1, dc, ch 2, dc, ch 1, dc) in every corner ch-2 sp and ending final replicate at ** - 48 dc, 44 ch-1 sps and 4 corner chain 2 spaces. Unite with slip stitch in 3rd chain of flipping ch-4. Ch 1, flip.

Rnd 7: (right side) Single crochet in subsequent ch-1 sp, single crochet in every dc and in every ch-1 sp around, working (sc, ch 2, sc) in every corner ch-2 sp and ending with single crochet in similar ch as uniting – 100 sc and 4 corner chain 2 spaces. Unite with slip stitch in last sc. Do not flip.

Rnd 8: Ch 1, single crochet in subsequent sc; *sk subsequent 2 sc, shell in subsequent sc, sk subsequent 2 sc**, single crochet in subsequent sc; replicate from * around, working (shell in corner ch-2 sp, single crochet in subsequent sc) in every corner and ending final replicate at ** - 20 shells and 20 sc. Unite with slip stitch in beginning sc. Flip.

Rnd 9: (wrong side) Slip stitch in subsequent 2 dc, slip stitch in subsequent dc (center dc of shell), ch 1, single crochet in similar dc; *shell in subsequent sc, single crochet in center dc of subsequent shell; replicate from * around, working (shell in sc, sk subsequent dc, single crochet in subsequent dc, shell in subsequent dc (center dc of shell), single crochet in subsequent dc, skip subsequent dc, shell in sc) in every corner – 24 shells and 24 sc. Unite with slip stitch in beginning sc. Ch 5 (counts as double crochet and chain-2 sp on subsequent round), flip.

Rnd 10: (right side) Single crochet in center dc of subsequent shell, ch 2; *dc in subsequent sc, ch 2, single crochet in center dc of subsequent shell, ch 2; replicate

Working [dc in subsequent sc, chain 2, sk subsequent dc, dc in subsequent dc, ch 1, (dc, chain 2, dc) in subsequent dc, ch 1, dc in subsequent dc, chain 2, skip subsequent dc] in every corner – 40 dc, 20 sc, 52 ch- 2 sps and 8 ch-1 sps. Unite with slip stitch in 3rd chain of beginning ch-5. Do not flip.

Rnd 11: Ch 1, single crochet in similar ch as uniteing, single crochet in every st and in every ch-1 sp, operating 2 single crochet in every ch-2 sp and (sc, chain 2, sc) in every corner ch-2 sp – 172 sc. Unite with slip stitch in beginning sc. Ch 1, flip.

Rnd 12 (wrong side): Single crochet in subsequent sc; *ch 1, sk subsequent sc**; single crochet in subsequent sc; replicate from * around, working (sc, chain 2, sc) in every corner ch-2 sp and ending final replicate at ** - 92 sc, 88 ch-1 sps and 4 corner chain 2 spaces. Unite with slip stitch in beginning sc. Fasten off. Weave all ends.

Subsequent back work to be done similar as front.

WEAVE RIBBONS:

Weave ribbons on face of pillow as follows:

Weave shorter length of green ribbon inside and outside of ch sps on round 3. Weave purple ribbon inside and outside of ch sps on round 6.

Weave longer length of green ribbon inside and outside of ch sps on round 10. Trim ribbons as required. Sew ends of ribbons tog on wrong side of pillow front.

Fabric pillow cover

Taking right sides of fabric collectively, sew seam with ½" seam allowance on 3 sides of pillow using needle and thread. Trim corners and flip fabric right side outside. Pop in pillow form. Flip under left behind edges of fabric ½" to wrong side and sew closed.

JOINING:

With wrong sides of facing and rear tog and front facing, work throughout both thicknesses as follows:

Slot in hook in foremost ch-1 sp to left of corner ch-2 sp and draw up a lp, ch 1, single crochet in similar sp; *ch 1, sk next sc**; single crochet in subsequent ch-1 sp; replicate from * all around, operating (sc, chain 2, sc) in every corner ch-2 sp and ending final repeat at **.

Work around 3 sides of pillow; put in covered pillow form and complete last side – 96 sc, 92 ch-1 sps and 4 corner chain 2 spaces. Fasten together with slip stitch in beginning sc. tie off and Weave all ends.

Final Steps

Then prepare four yarn tassels in the following manner:

- Twist yarn all around cardboard for approximately fifteen times.
- Enclose 10" per 25.4cm piece of yarn all around wound yarn at one end of cardboard and tie a knot. Trim the other end of yarn and do away with from cardboard.
- Wind 10" piece of yarn several times around wound yarn, approximately ½"/1.3cm from tied end, fasten a granny knot and spruce ends.
- Fasten tassels to four corners of pillow by means of 10" tied end. Finally weave all ends.

Design no. 10

Essentials:

- Yarn: Balls of two different desired colors
- Crochet Hook of size 4mm [US G-6].
- Needle of yarn,
- Size of 12" pillow form.
- GAUGE: 15 sts = 4"

Method:

To alter Color in Sc:

Go through last st before changing color until 2 lps are left on hook, jump through color in use, gap up next color to be used and sketch through 2 lps on hook.

Continue with new color. Hold color which is not in use against wrong side of work, working above the strand for every 3 or 4 sts.

Rear:

With CA, ch 46.

Row 1 (work from Right Side): Single crochet in 2nd ch from hook and in every ch crossways and go round – 45 sc.

Row 2: Chain 1, single crochet in every sc crosswise; flip.

Replicate Row until 12" from beg. Fasten off.

FRONT:

With CA, ch 46.

Row 1 : Single crochet in 2nd ch as of hook and in every ch across; flip – 45 sc.

Row 2: Chain 1, single crochet in every sc across; flip.

Rows 3-10: Ch 1, single crochet in primary 2 sc with CA, * single crochet in subsequent 8 sc with CB, single crochet in subsequent 3 sc with CA; replicate from * across ending with 2 sc of CA as an alternative of 3; flip.

Rows 11-14: Replicate Row 2 with CA.

Rep Rows 3-14 two more times, then rep Rows 3-12 once more. Tie off and weave all ends.

Front Edging:

With right side in front of every other, connect CA in any sc; ch 1, work sc evenly around complete front, working 3 single crochet in every corner; fasten together with a slip stitch to first sc. Work 1 more round sc. tie off.

FINISHING:

With wrong sides together, sew pillow rear and front together leaving one side open. Place in pillow form and sew side closed.

ABBREVIATIONS:

beg = beginning; CA, CB = color A, B; ch = chain; rep = repeat; sc = single crochet; * = repeat whatever follows the * as indicated, mm = millimeters.

Conclusion

These were some of the mentioned designs. They would have definitely broadened your expertise. And now with application of some knowledge and tactics, you will be able to implement more and more designs in your cushion making.

Made in United States
Troutdale, OR
06/19/2025

32255442R00077